# THEATRE AND FRIENDSHIP

HENRY JAMES

# THEATRE
# AND FRIENDSHIP

## SOME
## HENRY JAMES
## LETTERS

WITH A COMMENTARY BY

ELIZABETH ROBINS

*Select Bibliographies Reprint Series*

BOOKS FOR LIBRARIES PRESS
FREEPORT, NEW YORK

First Published 1932
Reprinted 1969

STANDARD BOOK NUMBER:
8369-5156-5

LIBRARY OF CONGRESS CATALOG CARD NUMBER:
73-103656

PRINTED IN THE UNITED STATES OF AMERICA

My *special acknowledgments are due to Henry James, Junior, for his permission to publish his uncle's letters. Lady Richmond for her kindness in allowing me to include certain letters from Henry James to Lady Bell, and Doctor Wilberforce for lending her picture of Hilda with Lady Bell's lettering for reproduction, I have also to thank.*

*Those interested in Mr. Henry James whether as novelist or dramatist will, I think, be glad to know of the two volumes of scholarly research and faithful documentation recently published by M. Léon Edel,* Henry James, Les Années Dramatiques *and* The Prefaces of Henry James. *These highly interesting works were lent to me by Mme. de Navarro [Mary Anderson] too late to be the help they might have been since* Theatre and Friendship *was already in the publishers' hands.*

E. R.

OF the memorable things Henry James has to say about letters — and there are many in 'Notes of a Son and Brother' — nothing needs more to be recalled, in an unbraced age, than a passage out of the chapter dedicated to a love of his early days, the cousin who died young. Before quoting the vivid pages she wrote to another man, he says:

*Needless enough surely to declare that such pages were essentially not love-letters: that they could scarce have been less so seems exactly part of their noble inevitability, as well as a proof singularly interesting and charming that confident friendship may obey its force and insist on its say quite as much as the sentiment we are apt to take, as to many of its occasions, for the supremely vocal. We have so often seen this latter beat distressfully about the bush for something still deficient, something in the line of positive esteem or constructive respect, whether offered or enjoyed, that an esteem and a respect such as we here apprehend, explicit enough on either side to dispense with those superlatives in which graceless reaction has been known insidiously to lurk, peculiarly refresh and instruct us. The fine special quietude of the relation thus promoted in a general consciousness of unrest — and even if it could breed questions too, since a relation that breeds none at all is not a living one — was of the highest value to the author of my letters, who had already sufficiently 'lived,' in her generous way, to know well enough in how different a quarter to look for the grand inconclusive. The directness, the ease, the extent of the high consideration, the felt need of it as a support, indeed one may almost say as an inspiration, in trouble, and the free gift of it as a delightful act of intelligence and justice, render the whole exhibition, to my sense, admirable in its kind.*

# CONTENTS

# ILLUSTRATIONS

# THEATRE
# AND FRIENDSHIP

# INTRODUCTORY

THERE has been some question as to whether out of the hundred and fifty-odd letters and notes written to me by Mr. Henry James — and now for the first time brought together — there are enough of sufficient interest to others to make a small volume.

The original idea was to publish a selection of the letters as they stand without comment. The outcome of talks and correspondence on the subject, between Mr. James's namesake-nephew and myself, has made clear his feeling that without certain connective links and elucidations the letters would fail of their proper significance.

'... you to whom the letters are addressed ...' writes the younger Henry James, 'read them with a warmer mind and a richer accompaniment of associations than will anyone else ... without guidance comparatively few others will catch the implications with which you are familiar of old and which seem to you to stare one in the face. ...' He goes on to suggest that I should 'evoke a ... background.'

The only one who could do that would be the author of the letters. The best I can do is to turn to them for such suggestions as they can offer.

On reacquaintance I have found in these pages two things. First: a record of Mr. James's preoccupation with the theatre — apart from his personal adventure as a playwright — which, so far as I know, has been confessed nowhere else. There is evidence of his knowledge of plays, playwrights and acting, not only English — a knowledge wide, often intimate and not without possibilities of service to the English theatre. Into this category falls a curious revelation that must be of interest to students of letters: I mean the fluctuating influence, on that particular mind, of the early Ibsen invasion; how the inevitable hostility broke down completely at one point and another, showing the strength in Mr. James of the sheer theatre-sense and his loyalty to it; his unwilling, his passionately unwilling, but frank and generous capitulation to Ibsen's '... intensity, his vividness, the hard compulsion of his strangely inscrutable art.'

Mr. James's openness of mind to dramatic values, wherever he found them, is further shown in his eager acceptance of Echegaray's 'Mariana' and still more in his whole-hearted readiness to fling himself into the serious-enough task of giving that fine thing out of Spain a fitting English dress.

The appeal made to Mr. James by the theatre has been deprecated and as much as possible dropped out of sight by his friends, by the general reader, and by all those who, so far as I know, have written about him. That he himself again and again raged against the spell cast on him by the stage — is only another proof of the inveterate strength of his natural predilection. That predilection, as I may be able to make clear, survived long after he was believed to have thankfully forgotten it. For the truth was, he thankfully remembered — as at least one of the 'Mariana' letters will show. Naturally, so incor-

16

rigible a love for the theatre, and so unrewarded a fidelity to its interests, was admitted only to the one or two as unrepentant as himself.

Letter No. 79 to Lady Bell emphasizes the persistence of Henry James's concern for the Theatre. Apart from the light it sheds on his eager recognition of dramatic promise, his angry protest against its neglect and discouragement, the letter shows how ready he would have been, after he had abandoned any hope of reward to himself, to put his stores of knowledge and his critical power at the service of the English stage.

Those who saw Mr. William Archer's first draft of a National Theatre Scheme will be reminded of the important part assigned to an advisory board, with artists, men of letters, tous les talents willing to lend their enthusiasm and expert knowledge to the Playhouse. On such a board Mr. James would have pleaded a fair hearing should be given, if only by way of encouragement to further work from two men whose prentice hands could produce 'Admiral Guinea.'

But apart from any question of literature, or the stage, the letters from the merely human point of view have a contribution to make that cannot, I think, be common.

Let it be said at once that what is presented here bears no comparison with the letters already published by Mr. Percy Lubbock: those voluminous, considered communications, on subjects, as I readily admit of more general interest, written in great part after Mr. James's retirement to the country and intended to take the place of personal intercourse.

I have included a number out of many more of the mere notes passing between people within easy reach and often meeting. Some of these are given place because Mr. James could apparently write nothing that did not bear the stamp of temperament or style. Who ever strewed the accents of speech so freely about in a telegram as he in answer to Lady Bell's invitation to Yorkshire:

> 'Impossible impossible impossible if you knew what it costs me to say so you can count however at the regular rates ask Miss Robins to share your regret I mean mine
>
> Henry James'

Or to me — an invitation to 'a rude lunch,' or to dine with him 'very slightly' before the play, on 'chicken and fixings.' Or: '...I will look out for you this evening at the Theatre door — to "arm" you in — up to 8 o'clock when I will, failing your visibility, seek the security of the box.'

I see him again standing there, anxious, solicitous, and then being gaily claimed, seeking in haste 'the security of the box.' I see him listening warily to the play, or in an entr'acte to his companion, with that look all of us, not least his devoted friends, came to know — the look of silent inward laughter; a laughter never with safety to be interpreted as with, but *at* something or somebody, probably the one nearest.

The other reason I have come to think some of those notes might be retained is because they, as much as any, illustrate the second thing that came out to meet me on re-reading: that here is the light-running, long-continued record of an unusual type of friendship. I know of nothing that shows clearer Mr. James's genius for 'sharing' or his power of un-stinted service — not the least part being a criticism

18

sensitive, shrewd, humorous, and, behind all, an exquisite kindness derived straight from that period of his most passionate preoccupation with the stage.

It went through many alien forms, this spirit of friendship, but it never faltered. It made itself at home, as the letters show, in the haunts of Adelphi melodrama. It made him welcome with an ardour that astonishes even me a play devoted to justification of Militant Woman-Suffrage (page 262) that agitation so antipathetic to his character and taste. It reached out as far as to the Klondyke.

Looking back, I find no assurance that I realized at anything like their full value the treasures of wisdom, genius and sensitive participation that Mr. James brought to friendship. One of the things about life hardest to accept is that most of us do not understand what is happening *while* it is happening. There is an effect of malice in that law by which our nearest approach to clear-seeing comes only with the backward look.

But like him I too, am glad to remember those 'Mariana' evenings and those varied tea-time sessions. Perhaps perversely, one most of all — seeing him to the door one particular evening, and coming out with him on the open-air landing. Henry James standing there above the seventy-four stone steps, looks down, looks up, looks round; meditative, melancholy.

'This — is — er — is like —'

I wondered uneasily, what *is* it 'like' in those sophisticated eyes? Yet wasn't the sunset doing its best to help Manchester Square Mansions and me to make a 'good show'? — wasn't the light sifting crimson and gold over the black roofs and chimneys and down the long flights of stone?

I haven't the ghost of a remembrance of trying to divert him from bringing out some comparison too little flattering, but, remembering Henry James, I almost think I may have quoted somebody's obliging suggestion that my abode had something 'foreign' about it.

'Certainly . . . it has — er — er — a *quality*, this place — er —' a longer check and then the deep voice boomed: 'It is like *Morocco!*'

To the accompaniment of my delighted laughter, he went on down while I remembered my first night here; coming home to this unfinished building after my first meeting with Mr. James — feeling my way up those stairs in the unlit dark, in the ice and snow.

'Oh, exactly like Morocco!' I called down.

Indoors, I wondered, as I still do, what did Mr. James know about Morocco? As little as about me — for he had complained to Florence Bell that I had too little ambition.

But I am glad of the reminder (in the Stevenson-Henley letter) that I once stood up before Henry James and recited my 'piece' like a school-child before The Master.

And that it happened in Morocco.

There is good reason for my associating this book with the name of Florence Bell, yet it seems that, too, 'needs explaining.'

It is some fifteen years since Mr. James left the scene. But Lady Bell was moving quick and vivid among us so recently — writing and godmothering her great Yorkshire Pageant; editing the letters of her step-daughter Gertrude Bell; occupying her place in the front row on London First Nights — that I feel it a blow to the continuity of life itself to be told she is already little known to the general public and not known at all (as Henry James and I knew her longest) under the name of Mrs. Hugh Bell. She can never have been more perfectly described in a few words than by Mr. James himself when he wrote to her in 1912 as 'lady of the full programme and the rich performance.'

I have never lived close to a woman of so many gifts and interests. To one of these only — the one she shared with Mr. James — I propose to make here what cannot be more than inadequate reference.

Though they never met till the late 'eighties, the childhood and early youth of both Henry James and Florence Bell were spent in France. This circumstance was an important element in the bond between them.

On her part, interest in the Stage dated from a period so early that she was probably the very youngest frequenter the Théâtre Français ever knew, certainly, I should say, the youngest of English blood — or, as in her case, Irish-English. One would like to know just what infant signs of passion for the play induced that remarkable personage, her father Sir Joseph Olliffe, to choose the next to youngest of his three small daughters to be his constant companion in the box at the Français, commonly placed at his disposal.

Though this early appetite of hers was later starved through a long stretch of time (long, as youth measures deprivation) the appetite was never lost and never sated. In later life, at rare intervals, she would turn out of a deep drawer piles of evidence that, during those years when she lived out of reach of the theatre, she had again and again been trying her hand at the dramatic form — with undis-

21

courageable joy. So it was that, in those country years, she passed from the little plays, French and English — that she began to write for her children when they were hardly more than babies — through one period of Fairy Tale plays, and to another of Chamber Comedies. As time went on, from more ambitious dramatic work (little, if any, produced; most of it never even 'offered') she passed at a bound to the comedy 'L'Indécis,' accepted and played by the greatest actor in France.

She recalls this success of hers and Coquelin's in a letter written in 1892 after sending me her translation of a play from the German. At this particular moment she was turning into French a play of her own which I was to send with a beautiful letter — not of my own composing — to Sarah Bernhardt. That my friend might be called on any day for help in turning the 'Master Builder' out of Norwegian into speakable stage English, was in her eyes some compensation for allowing Ibsen, or any other, to come in the way of our very own play. This last, our work of collaboration, her letter calls 'Befriad' and our 'find.' It is so referred to by Henry James.

Mrs. Hugh Bell wrote in the letter already quoted:

'It is an auspicious anniversary for me to-day — Thursday 10th, 1887, was my first venture — the first night of the "Indécis." Five years ago! — sometimes I think it's a long time to have been at it — at others I say to myself it isn't really very long when one hears tales of other people's years of hopeless struggle — and I don't think I ever felt hopeless. I was certainly started with a good spurt — I shall never forget that morning afterwards . . . when I was

22

so foolish and inexperienced I didn't even look with certainty to there being any notices of it [Coquelin's production of "L'Indécis"] — and then coming down and finding the papers one burst of surprise and gratulation — it *was* good!'

In the same letter she adjures me to keep her 'au courant. And even though you are driving all this furious team of things abreast, snatch a moment every now and again to send me a scrap. Oh, I wonder what you said to H[enry] J[ames] last night about your "find"— *find!* ha, ha! and how very very glad I am that it ["Alan's Wife"] hadn't got back into your hands yet, so that you couldn't show it to him. Oh, don't let him throw cold water on it.' She adds, characteristically, 'If I heard — (which I cannot expect) that you told him the plot and that he was struck by it, I shall not be able to help feeling hopeful. I've just accomplished an eloquent letter to Sarah B. It's very interesting writing to geniuses, and I should like to keep my hand in — so here goes! Oh, I do wonder what Tree will say to you, and you to him to-day, about 'Sie ist Wahnsinnig; Gewirrwigs'— perhaps 'Befriad': I hardly think Stella.* Isn't life interesting! it is, it is! . . .'— and she meant the life of the stage, she who had seen life in so many of the capitals of Europe and had chosen for her own that remote Yorkshire life of the home.

In old age, as in youth, she could win hearts in all the known ways. She could win my Theatre-heart in ways known to nobody else. 'I love the very *smell* of Behind-the-Scenes,' she said once, snuffing it up her fine high nose. By which confession she proved I was not the only one who felt the spell of that old queer aroma, unknown to pampered

* Mrs. Hugh Bell had dramatized the story of Swift.

players in the antiseptic haunts of to-day, that exciting, intensely evocative smell — Araby itself is
insufficiently blest without it! — the commingled
odours of rank-dank, of dust, paint, and escaping
gas.

She claimed 'as one of us' the father of our friend,
her 'dear Annie Ritchie's' father, on the strength of
his challenge to some superior person: Whether he
really cared about the Theatre. 'You aren't much
for it,' Thackeray insisted. 'Oh, yes, I like a *good*
play.' 'Go along! you don't know what we are talking about,' said the delightful, understanding man.

Florence Bell was the first to show me how much
the actor may learn from the non-professional. All
but the very greatest people of the stage come early
to accept the conventional makeshifts. Actors will
outrage probability, they will defeat their own best
effects, all for lack of the unsophisticated eye. Few
people, I think, who are truly sensitive to the theatrical atmosphere can ever be quite at ease watching
a scene where there is a baby. They are suspicious
even of a cradle in a far corner. If there's a real baby
concealed there, who can think of the play for
anxiety as to what will happen when real life 'takes
the stage'? This dreadful danger of some effect not
down in the prompt book has brought about a meek
acceptance of practically any makeshift. The idea
seems to be, since to have a real baby is to court
perdition, it doesn't matter how unreal is the substitute. But this, too, is ruinous. There must be
many who never see the swathed stiffness of the
theatre doll without a sense of jar. I preferred, but
Mrs. Hugh Bell revolted against, the armful of
shawls that I rehearsed with in the big scene of her
translation of 'Karen.' 'You *can't* hold a bundle of

24

rags as you'd hold a child —' she complained. 'The
bundle must have bones.' So after rehearsal I was
carried off to find the bones.

In those days there was an artist's shop with a
French name in the Regent Street Quadrant. Mrs.
Hugh Bell had been accustomed to go in, soberly,
and ask for canvas and colours, or the mere pencil
of a person for whom a pencil is not a thing with a
point that makes some sort of mark, but a creative
implement of infinite variety and every degree of
aid or disobligingness. I see, now, the decently
curbed surprise of the man at the pencil-counter,
when the respected customer flew in and demanded
an articulated model, not of a grown person and not
quite an infant.

Thereupon a brisk scene: Mrs. Hugh Bell enlist-
ing interest in her enterprise; premises overhauled;
pencilman, turned ally, finds the useable size '— and
to what address, Madam?' Madam's 'We can't wait —
we'll take it!' precipitates the ally into another rôle
— the kind but very self-conscious porter bearing
into the street and stowing in our hansom a third
occupant, insufficiently clothed in brown paper —
the child I was to carry dead out of my husband's
house in the last act. It was so I came to realize how
much that scene owed to the fact that the mother's
wild grief was not wasted over a boneless bundle.
This was the first of a long series of interventions
that illustrate the theatre-sense which Mrs. Hugh
Bell shared with Henry James — and with Charles
Dickens.

Sybil Thorndike reminds me of our being told
how Dickens begged Florence Bell's mother not to
bar the little schoolgirl from coming to the first of
those famous Readings of his in Paris. He *had* to

25

have Florence there — she was 'such a good audience.'

And not less good for tragedy than for comedy. I have said elsewhere that my early friendship with her was founded on the circumstance of her being the one person who, not of the theatre, yet loved and understood the theatre beyond any other I had known. It was amazing to see the quickness with which she responded to the less tangible, less communicable influences of the most elusive of the arts. It seemed to me, that first night Duse played in London, she played to Florence Bell; no other member of the general public in all that spell-bound audience did the magic of the great Italian reach so surely; while the subtlest look, the most delicate intonation, played on her as airs upon a wind-harp; she felt the supreme achievement as one had thought only the passionate student and disciplined player could feel.

Certainly among all Mr. James's acquaintances he could have found nobody in 1891 so knowledgeable about the theatre, home and foreign, as Mrs. Hugh Bell. It was the most natural thing in the world for him to write asking her if she had read 'Hedda Gabler.'

Not as easily accounted for was his habit of associating her with my doings from the Hedda days onward. I am quite sure he never heard her call me as she did quite early 'min lille söster.' Yet the instancy of Henry James's recognition of 'relationship,' the delicate sureness of his acceptance, were never more clearly shown than in his 'placing' of this figure in the life of his newly transplanted compatriot. It was as if he could see from the beginning that of the two small parts Florence Bell had cast herself for in the great repertory of her life, the first was: to be my Blest Companion in a castle in the air; and the second, one of whom it could be said, as Carlyle said of his friend: 'She furnished the English earth and made it homelike to me!'

CHAPTER I

# BEGINNINGS

I met Mr. James in January 1891.

On the same day I had been rehearsing my first Ibsen part, Mrs. Linden, in 'A Doll's House,' about to be revived for a single performance. Some days after that first meeting, my friend Miss Geneviève Ward wrote to me: 'I gave Mr. James my second ticket for the matinée — he wished to see the play — strange.'

That performance certainly did not lessen his unwilling interest in Ibsen. On the same date he wrote to Mrs. Hugh Bell asking her if she had come across the play 'Hedda Gabler.' I ought to say he was not referring to the translation which was used later for stage production and which was practically the same as the one printed in Mr. William Archer's final edition of Ibsen.

'Read it,' Mr. James advised Mrs. Hugh Bell — 'for its strange mixture of pointless flatness and convincing *life*. Also of desolate untheatricality and dramatic ingenuity.'

The play so described was already occupying Marion Lea and me and a considerable number of other people. Miss Lea was a young Phila-

29

delphian of much natural distinction and cosmopolitan education, already favourably known on the London stage. She lived with her half sister, Mrs. Lea Merritt, the painter, who had built herself a charming studio-house in Tite Street where Mr. James was on dining terms.

Almost from the first, Marion Lea and I had Mr. William Heinemann with us in our project of putting 'Hedda Gabler' on the stage. Mr. Heinemann was not only the singularly enlightened publisher of the play, he was owner of the theatrical rights. In spite of adverse notices (the published play had met a storm of obloquy and derision) Mr. Heinemann was determined 'Hedda Gabler' should be given a hearing. To this end, he had entered into certain commitments with other people — among them Mr. Justin Huntly McCarthy — before we appeared on the scene. After negotiations, some of them calm, some much the reverse, with various translators and aspirants for stage rights, Marion Lea and I were about to produce 'Hedda Gabler' at a series of matinées.

So it was that, some two and a half months after Mr. James had advised Mrs. Hugh Bell to go so far as to read 'Hedda Gabler,' he was writing what may possibly be his first letter to me. It is dated 'Monday,' from 34 De Vere Gardens. '... I shall be present in force at your première — I take the greatest interest in your enterprise and am extremely glad it takes such good form. I hope you have some intelligent men. I am, at any rate. (Excuse that, 'at any rate'— I sometimes doubt if there are any intelligent men!) I shall be eager to see you in a part of real capacity and am most truly yours, Henry James.'

Before the letter of May 29th, and accounting for its being written, comes the circumstance that the 'Hedda Gabler' matinées led to offers of engagement from Messrs. Gatti of the Adelphi, Thorne of the Vaudeville, John Hare and Charles Wyndham — besides those direct negotiations with Mr. Henry Arthur Jones to which the letter specially refers.

If not *the* reason, one reason why greater use was not made of these opportunities will appear later in Mr. James's criticism of my way of conducting my affairs.

## I

34 *De Vere Gardens, W.*
May 29th [1891]

Dear Miss Robins.

I am greatly hoping that you will kindly agree to see my friend Edward Compton, who was with me last night at the Vaudeville, on the subject of such possibilities as may exist of your doing Mme. de Cintré in my 'American' on its production here in September next. He was exceedingly interested, of course, in your Hedda, and I have undertaken to ask him, on your behalf if you can give him half an hour either on *Sunday, Tuesday,* or *Wednesday* — preferably in the afternoon: no matter how early. He would be delighted to come and see you, or if you are away from home at those hours I should be delighted, that he should meet you *here* — when you can have the place to yourselves. Will you kindly address a word directly to him —

Edward Compton, Esq.
54 Avonmore Road,
Kensington, W.?

mentioning such time as will suit you and to which he will conform? — I have been hoping for some news of you ever since the day I last saw you — when you expected to clear up the prospect of Henry Arthur [Jones]. I am *now* hoping that it is sufficiently clearer for you to take some little interest in *us* — even if on the basis of simply *starting* us in the early autumn if H.A. is to come on (as would seem probable) in the later. You can desert us for him on the day he wants you.

Yours most truly
Henry James

Mr. James's hand is evident, ten days later, in the formal offer of engagement written by his Manager and leading actor, Mr. Edward Compton. It differed in one respect from the usual Theatrical contract which stipulated that even when the actor was not needed at his own theatre, under no circumstances should he appear professionally in any other.

Marion Lea and I had seen how materially an actor's prospects might be affected by playing at occasional matinées. We had promised each other to do our utmost to reserve the right of playing elsewhere on afternoons when the piece for which we were specially engaged was not being

32

performed. At that time such a proposal was regarded by the regular London Managers with
more than suspicion and disfavour. It was down-
right revolutionary; but Mr. James supported us
in this demand, and I signed under my own conditions.

In view of the note of June 16th and still more
in view of many of Mr. James's later letters, it is
clear that Mr. Henry James the Younger is right.
His uncle's interest in Marion Lea and me must
be explained.

It should therefore be said that the success of
'Hedda Gabler' had changed the face of the London world for Mr. James's young compatriots.
Yet, however much we might seem to be justified
in expecting from the regular Theatre, the
regular Theatre could not content us. The
further result of the reception given to 'Hedda
Gabler' was to encourage Miss Lea and me in
a hope that haunted our dreams before we
ever heard of 'Hedda'— a hope of escape from
need to accept the conditions of the existing
Theatre.

We had come to realize how essential to success some freedom of judgment and action are to
the actor. The strangulation of this rôle and that
through arbitrary stage management, was an experience we had shared with men. But we had
further seen how freedom in the practice of our
art, how the bare opportunity to practise it
at all, depended, for the actress, on considerations
humiliatingly different from those that con-
fronted the actor. The stage career of an actress
was inextricably involved in the fact that she was
a woman and that those who were masters of the

theatre were men. These considerations did not belong to art; they stultified art.

We dreamed of an escape, through hard work, and through deliberate abandonment of the idea of making money — beyond what would give us the wages of going on. We would organize a season — leading up to future seasons — of that Lea-Robins Joint Management, so dear to our hearts, that had already seen 'Hedda' through. The full houses, the kind of people who helped to fill them, buoyed up our hope that not only followers but active helpers would gather round the new Standard. As time went on, more and more of the public would be fired by the still unexplored possibilities of the theatre. If it was true as someone over there in France had said, all that is needed for a play is two boards and a passion, why should the effects we longed to produce be prejudiced by our spending a mere fraction of what stage-setting cost other theatres? We wouldn't be able to afford advertising. What of that? Other people, 'our public,' who cared about this new kind of theatre, must advertise it. Given a little time, the perfection of the company must advertise it. With the same passion of care we had given to the much-praised 'Hedda' cast, we would choose and keep together a permanent nucleus — making now and then special engagements as fresh plays might require. Actors were coming to realize that 'Ibsen made reputations.' Not Ibsen alone, we were sure. We would gather actors about us who would often be playing bigger parts than our own. We would attract the more intelligent player by a variety of dramatic opportunity that no theatre dependent on the

34

long run could offer. We felt sure we were not the only acting folk who found an intensity of happiness in *working together* at interesting stuff. Others would be glad to take salaries as modest as our own for joy of the new work and the glory of the new aim.

Much of this untamed optimism we, naturally, spared Mr. James, but we told him that we intended the Joint Management to continue. As to material, apart from revivals of English plays, at the beginning we would modestly draw the best out of the repertories of every capital in Europe. In time, new first-rate English plays would come our way. Those people who ought to be in the service of the theatre and who still remained outside it, must be brought in. If French and German men of letters wrote for the stage, why shouldn't the English? Still in the future were not only the plays of Oscar Wilde and Bernard Shaw, but Anthony Hope's enormously popular 'Prisoner of Zenda,' Langdon Mitchell's fortune-coining 'New York Idea,' and his dramatization of 'Becky Sharp,' and Du Maurier's 'Trilby.' But we could point, at least with the finger of hope, to George Meredith as one of those, cap in hand before the Théâtre Français, who said he never went to the play in London — yet had come to see 'Hedda Gabler.' So had Thomas Hardy. Oh, the novelists would help, the publishers would help. Had not Mr. William Heinemann already done wonders for us? And was he not going to move heaven and earth to secure the next Ibsen?'

We would enlist the poets, the new as well as the old, and not only those who were dramatists. The very ballad-monger should not escape us.

35

We had a scheme of making a sublime curtain-raiser, or an after-piece (climax to some rare evening out of Rossetti's ballad of 'Sister Helen.' For sake of his Pre-Raphaelite Brother why shouldn't Burne-Jones (I am far from sure he had yet heard of the project) but why shouldn't he design a medieval setting for the Little Brother and the pale avenging woman? — those two wonderful parts that must be acted to musical accompaniment. Yes, music, to carry the recurrent burden of the verse — music as right and rare as the poetry! Hadn't we friends who might even ask Grieg to write this music? And why shouldn't he — for Rossetti?

It will be seen there was nothing we did not aspire to, or expect of our friends. Mr. James did not blench. He not only met the full impact of this spring flood with patience. He positively urged it on. Probably his recognition of Marion Lea's highly original and finished talent for comedy led him to contemplate helping the Joint Management by doing a play for us himself.

## II

34 *De Vere Gardens, W.*
June 16th [1891]

Dear Miss Robins.

Would any day next week — from the 22nd to the 26th, both inclusive, suit you to come here at 4 p.m. and hear, in a pure artistic spirit 2 acts of the 3-Act Comedy we had some talk of? (I say 2 acts because I fear No. 3 would have — will have — to become the subject of an occasion by itself — it is the pièce de résistance.) If you will pick out an afternoon that suits both you and Miss Lea, I will write to Miss Lea — and will also ask L. Mitchell to come. If next week shouldn't suit you — perhaps the following would. I hope the flat is flattening out.

Yours most truly

Henry James

No one realized more perfectly than Mr. James that the plan of the Joint Management necessitated not merely the acquiring of this or that particular play, but the building up of a Repertory. We hoped to make a fair beginning at this before we again challenged public attention.

With the single exception of the Lyceum, all London Theatres in those days subsisted in great part on plays from the French. Why, then, might not the Joint Management so subsist till our more fruitful hour should come?

The French play must of course be good of its kind and promise a chance to make reputation. Mr. James's years of Theatre-going in Paris had made him a library of dramatic reference. We, of course, went to the library. But whether he himself suggested Dumas, among the many French dramatists he brought under review, seems unlikely, judging from what he writes about 'Denise.' His reference to Clement Scott's abbreviation of the play in English form suggests a likely source of our information.

By whatever route when, in the course of our search, Marion Lea and I came on 'Denise' in the original, we said at once: This is what we want. Marion Lea was willing to undertake the second part if I would do 'Denise.' IF I would!

We knew nothing about the history of the play beyond what Mr. James told us. Probably not even Mr. James knew that when Dumas had finished it he sent a copy to his (and Mr. James's) friend, Count Primoli, with a request that it might be shown to the new Italian actress Primoli had talked about. I did not know till the other day that, forty years ago, this Dumas play which on such reasoned grounds Mr. James had urged us to abandon, and which in spite of all that he could say we clung to so tightly, had appealed to the greatest actress of the age 'more intimately' than anything she had ever played. 'No other part had seemed so naturally intended for her.' No other had so moved her since, at fourteen, she had played Juliet. In her beautiful hands, so Rheinhardt tells us, 'Denise' roused the Roman public to a frenzy. Even when they had left the Theatre, they could not bring themselves to go home. They filled the street shouting: 'Duse! Duse!'

It was a name not yet heard in England. All that we innocents knew in the summer of '91 was that we wanted to produce 'Denise' in English, and we wanted Mr. James to approve.

## III

34 *De Vere Gardens, W.*
June 25th [1891]

Dear Miss Robins.

Excuse a very brief and helpless scrawl from one who is only just feebly convalescent from a most horrid attack of influenza. I am discouraged in advance about 'Denise' — I mean for the simple reason that you will think I disapprove of *everything*. In as few words as possible my impression of 'Denise' is this:—It is, to my sense, a particularly big example of everything that the French audience patiently and interestedly accepts and that the English audience won't have ANYTHING to say to — i.e. the pièce à thèse, the long, analytic psychological, conversational *novel,* with action and movement reduced to their minimum, and discourse and the development of an idea raised to their maximum. It is intellectual, argumentative, slowly-moving, copious, full of shades and subtleties; whereas the only thing the English public will look at for a moment is the intensely simplified — the quick, instant, obvious, visible, tangible — the thing that jumps down your throat. 'Denise' is miles over their heads. I have seen it done twice at the Français, and each time with the sense 'How impossible in English!' I don't know what C.S.'s arrangement in 3 acts may be — and don't understand how a thing like 'Denise' — a work of art — can be chopped down, by a strange hand, at that rate and keep its quality. Don't play *any* play for the sake of *one* 'great scene': that way madness lies, and destruction, and death! And take well in account this — that there is a certain strong presumption against Dumas Fils inherent in the fact that he has had, save with the 'Dame aux Camélias,' *no* fortune on the English-speaking stage. The D. a.

C., a romantic play of his youth, was successful in America and Australia years ago, but is *never* produced in London. For the rest, London has always given the widest possible berth to the productions of his real career — and not a *single* one has found its way to the stage here; in spite of the poverty of said stage, the greatness of his position in France and the number of his pieces. This is a circumstance worth considering. The part of Marthe, I may add, would, it seems to me, be in the cut-down play, even less interesting to an English audience, than in the original. Let me add that I am taking a responsibility without knowing C.S.'s version — and that these are sickly, stammering words — I am still in very poor form. Ever yours and Miss Lea's

Henry James

Marion Lea and I had gone into retreat to read plays and plan our next 'Joint' move. Mr. James's letter of June 27th was forwarded to us at Broadstairs.

IV

34 De Vere Gardens, W.<br>June 27th [1891]

Dear Miss Robins.

I am afraid Balestier was too positive about my advent at Broadstairs or Margate. I am only thinking, vaguely, of getting *somewhere* to the sea, for a few days, as soon as I can leave town. I would come

40

and take a look at you at Margate with the greatest pleasure — *but* I have not yet been out of the house and I fear the doctor won't let me travel — even 2 or 3 hours — for four or five days yet. (I am absurdly weakened by 10 days of confinement with this horrid plague.) This, alas, would be just as you're returning to the arms of Buchanan, Sims & Co. However, I shall see you, I trust, at no distant day; for if I go away it will probably only be for a week. All the same I am sorry not to have the chance of revealing you the comedy by the sounding sea: a delightful programme. I wrote to you (41 M.H.) about 'Denise'. I fear you found me chilling — but I *do* see the idea very much in black. If I saw you I should be able to make all my reasons clear. When I do see you I will try. Since writing to you I have heard that Mme. Modjeska produced a version of the play in N.Y. a year or two ago with absolute non-success. If I had immediate clear command of my time *I* would engage to produce you 3 divine acts for your purpose. When do you regard your venture as likely to occur? I have for the next 3 months only fractions of time — but will ENDEAVOUR to have, within that period, a 1st act to read to you, on the chance.

Ever yours

Henry James

Marion Lea had left Broadstairs to finish her holiday abroad. I returned to London in fulfilment of an agreement made too early and too hastily, to play the heroine of the new melodrama at the Adelphi till — strange transition! — Mr. James's 'American' should be produced at the Opéra Comique on September 21st.

The growing depression of those midsummer rehearsals of 'The Trumpet Call' was mitigated by considering one play or another that might presently be grist in the Joint Management mill — also in considering, with Mrs. Edward Compton, the dresses for Mr. James's heroine.

## V

34 *De Vere Gardens, W.*
Wednesday

Dear Miss Robins.

Would Friday next suit you, if you have still the courage to listen to an act or two (there are three, but the third would have to be an occasion by itself,) of the irrespressible comedy? I have an idea you go out of town on Sunday — but if Friday is amiss, Saturday or Monday — or Tuesday or Wednesday next — would do equally for me. I confess however to preference for the earlier day! I mean for the pleasure of the thing and also for the greater allowance of time to follow with Act III — before the rehearsals of the American begin. And I would make it exactly the hour that suits you, as well as the place. 3? 4? Here? Dorset St.? Would either Friday or Saturday at 4 chez vous be the possible thing? Perhaps *Saturday* would be a *leetle* better for *me,* as I am spending awful hours with the dentist.

Yours most truly

Henry James

## VI

34 *De Vere Gardens, W.*

Friday

Dear Miss Robins.

That will do beautifully and I will be with you at 4 sharp to-morrow — straight from the Devil's Surgeon. I'm so glad Claire [the heroine of 'The American'] has 'good clothes'.

Yours most truly

Henry James

Word had come from the Adelphi managers insisting on the terms of my return.

## VII

34 *De Vere Gardens, W.*

Dear Miss Robins.

Bless you, I understand perfectly — and it is essentially true that the *London* success of my play *is* a blessing yet to be established. It isn't at all pre-determined by what happened in the country — and we must by all means regard it as contingent, as that will make us work the better. We shall *make*

43

it a triumph and break the heart of the Adelphi.—
I hope to be able to send you *to-day* the printed
prompt book — or at the furthest to-morrow.

Yours most truly
Henry James

Sept. 9th [1891]

Though we had not been able to relinquish the
hope of doing 'Denise,' Mr. James, at a time over-
full of his own stage affairs, was still trying to
find for us an alternative to Dumas, immediately
available for matinées.

VIII

*Athenæum Club,*
*Pall Mall, S.W.*

Dear Miss Robins — and dear Miss Lea.

I have found 2 copies of the 'Marquis de Villemer,'
after a vain hunt, before I found it, in every *other*
bookshop in town. I have only time to despatch
them to you — without refreshing my own recollection of the pieces — which dates from many years
ago — but which is very favourable. My *main*
hesitancy is on the ground of uncertainty as to the
value and interest of the part of the 2d younger
woman — who was (as I recollect), not Diane, the
ingénue, but Mme. d'Arglade. As to this you must
decide. You see there are 4 women in all — and
the part of the Marquise, as I remember it, very

44

good. You would have practically about the same sized cast as in 'Hedda'. I should think the two brothers might be done by the same men you had in mind for André and Ferdinand in 'Denise'. Miss —— (if you can stand her — *I* can't — don't leave this *about!*) would do the Marquise better probably than any one. But, oh BUT the formidable question of translation! I grieve to say I can't help you here. If I had command of my time now I would do it for you off-hand, quickly and beautifully — and for nothing — for your four Beaux Yeux: but I am, for the next month, in the tightest place, in the way of some pressing work, contracted for and unfinished, that I have ever been in my life. I shall be at the O.C. this evening. Ever both of yours.

Henry James

Saturday 12.20.
P.S. One thing is clear — that the play would demand *extreme* compression; and that a good English version will not be easy to come by. Ah, if you weren't in such a hurry! This is inauspicious! I mean your hurry.

H.J.

We had entered into negotiations with Clement Scott, the holder of the English rights in 'Denise'. He and Sydney Groundy were the chief theatrical translators and adaptors of the time. Sydney Grundy was the better and more expensive hand.

45

Clement Scott had the obvious advantage of being the most prominent of the dramatic critics, with the *Daily Telegraph* for his sounding board. Mr. Scott's word for or against a play or a player weighed with the managers incomparably more than anybody else's; it weighed even with Mr. James — though not in terms of credit, as can be seen in a later letter.

I do not know at what point we had arrived in our protracted efforts to secure 'Denise,' when Sir Augustus Harris came into the foreground — I should say *our* foreground, for he already loomed before the public not only as 'Lessee and Manager of The Theatre Royal, Drury Lane.' His appearance in the 'Denise' affair seems to have been designed to save Mr. Scott from the consequences of an agreement with us, or perhaps mainly from our persistent appeals that he should forgo his adaptation and do us a straight translation. Sir Augustus found no fault with the boiled-down Dumas. He proposed to give it no free-lance matinée trial, but a regular production at a regular Theatre, with, no doubt, a 'regular' cast. This plan did not, I think, materialize — perhaps was never meant to go further than the length of a life-saver to rescue Mr. Scott from the consequences of some too impulsive promise. That gentleman's natural-enough eagerness to place his adaptation in the hands of Sir Augustus Harris released us from any lingering sense of obligation to a form we deplored, and led to our inquiring into the legality of the right so to use Dumas.

Mr. James, or we, found that something like seven years had elapsed since 'Denise' had made her first appearance in Paris — long enough, we thought, for London to wait for her. So, taking our dramatic life in our hands, we planned to relieve Sir Augustus and the critic of the *Telegraph* of their supposed right to produce, at this time of day, their bastard version.

In spite of Mr. James's disapproval of our choice of play he did all in his power to clear up the legal obscurity for us. He invoked the help of his Agent of Genius. This was the long, fragile young American with the eager face, who had so quickly grappled to himself the almost idolatrous friendship of men whose confidence was not easy to capture.

We did not know that this Mr. Balestier (so appreciative of 'Hedda Gabler') was himself a writer, collaborating at that moment with the outstanding novelist of the day. Perhaps Mr. Rudyard Kipling did not yet foresee the extent of his future collaboration with the sister, Miss Balestier, so soon to become Mrs. Kipling, but it was no secret that Mr. James attributed to his 'very remarkable friend Wolcott' — 'remarkable services,' and that yet others, men of letters and publishers, looked on the young man as a kind of international liaison officer, though that term was not yet current in '91. We fully realized that Mr. James had carried our case of 'Denise' to the High Court of Appeal when he said he would 'ask Balestier.'

## IX

Dear Miss Robins.

I venture to enclose this fragment of a letter just received from Wolcott Balestier, though it settles nothing. It only constitutes a presumption — which as you see is not favourable to the idea of the lapse of an ownership of rights — through non-use. Excuse his calling your supposition weird, I am wiring him immediately and he will let me know the moment he has heard from [Bram] Stoker. — I am *haunted* by your difficulty and disappointment; and have been cudgelling my brains and memories to think of some right — absolutely right — thing from the French that you could take up. But, as yet I think only of wrong ones. Dumas Fils yields to my sense only the Princesse Georges, which has already been vulgarized — and which there are other reasons against. His magnificent 'Monsieur Alphonse' demands a magnificent middle-aged (that is 35) 'character actress' of a certain particular type and temperament; and has, with this, a charming younger woman's part. 'Les Idées de Mme Aubray' the same Jeannine would be a beautiful part for Miss Lea, but Mme Aubray is a woman of more than 40 — with a son of 22, or more. And then, for the British public, the *subject*! — *all* Dumas's subjects!! Beyond a certain point one hesitates. I ransack Octave Feuillet and Sardou — only to find tricky old romantic and artificial things of which the most feasible have been already Englished and the others are *un*feasible. So with my memories of other things in the contemporary French drama — long winded complicated impossibilities, or intensely local Parisian comedies presenting insurmountable difficulties. I have been trying this a.m. to put my hand on 'Les Corbeaux' by Henri Becq: played at the Théâtre Français 3 or 4 years ago and a most real and interesting thing. But I can't find it — I will look further this afternoon. If you and Miss Lea care to read it you will find it at Hachette's, King Wm. St., Charing X. (Théâtre de Henri Becq: 2 vols.) But I think I must have it — and will hunt. I will continue to think and think. Ah, what a pity *time* presses so — I wish that at the present moment — wish to heaven *I* had more. A highly successful 'American' would have given it to me; but as it is I must wait for it. I will send you 'Les Corbeaux' instantly if I find it; though, I confess I don't see *your* part in it.

Ever yours

H. James

[Part of Wolcott Balestier's letter to Henry James.]

... My mild contribution, in the shape of a telegraphic query, addressed to the learned Bram, will be made in the morning, when I shall have received his answer. He's naturally only at the theatre at night. My own impression, I must

49

tell you, meanwhile, though not definite, is certainly against Miss Robins's weird hypothesis. There may have been some such proviso before the Treaty of Berne; but since then everything is copyright just as much as if it were written in English by an Englishman; and Copyright remains Copyright fortunately, even if one chooses not to exercise its privileges for seven years, or for seventeen. At least it's true of books! Bram, however, is dealing in this sort of truck all the time, and knows the whole business down to the ground. For Miss Robins's sake I can only hope that the copyright in 'Denise' is as tight as a drum; and that Sir Augustus will remain obdurate.

[Mr. James adds: 'He thinks someone has contested Harris's ownership.']

## CHAPTER II

# THE AMERICAN

Several of Mr. James's 'Denise' letters were written while the London fortunes of 'The American' might be supposed to leave him no moment to think of anything else.

To the actor the contrast between the July rehearsals of the Sims-Buchanan melodrama and those of September for Mr. James's comedy of manners, was beyond any reach of imagining. Rehearsals of 'The American,' shot with anxiety as they were — as any important stage work must be — were full of an interest that 'all London', to our sense, seemed to share.

As for the atmosphere inside the Theatre, it is good to remember the consideration and — in this case, hardly less good to remember—the reticent curiosity shown by the company towards the author.

Some special curiosity there always must be, if only to see how the new-comer behind the scenes comports himself. Will he be the familiar, dumb fish-out-of-water? or will he insist on being partly the great public 'in front'; partly the Creator Behind All; or will he genially show himself in each

51

and every 'part' the Actor in Excelsis — irreparable loss to the Stage, making his appearance for this one shining hour?

That Mr. James was none of these, was, of course, not only because he had already been to one or two rehearsals of the country company. Into this first London Theatre of his practical acquaintance he came with no lack of confidence, but very quietly eager, intensely observant, gravely and happily 'there' to help us. We felt his approach to matters of the Stage to be fresh and exciting. We were flattered when he took trouble with us, more hopeful of ourselves. Even those who had little French of their own felt that Mr. James's reflected distinction on the enterprise. Certainly we had not heard anything comparable in other theatres. Someone — and I do wish I could be sure who — enlightened the rest of us, as to the 'suppleness' of our author's linguistic equipment. 'When he talks to George Moore — it is the French of the Academy. When he talks to Miss Dairolles [the 'Noémie' of our cast] it is French of the *coulisses*.' We felt, to be talked to as if you were a member of the Français gave Adrienne Dairolles an unfair advantage.

But it is not what the company thought of Mr. James, it is what he thought of the company that would be worth recording. I do not, of course, mean merely his despairing recognition of our utter inadequacy (with the probable exception of Miss Dairolles) to represent the people he had in mind. On rare occasions an author may see some character improved. Never, never, does he see the creature of his dreams. Though Mr. James must have suffered more acutely on this score than most (— than any?) he paid the 'loss on the exchange', of his ideal for our attempted realization, with patience and infinite courtesy.

Apart from the acting — an exception he would have smiled at wryly, but I make it in all good faith — Mr. James's enjoyment of those rehearsals was real enjoyment, at least while he was in the Theatre.

I cannot think he ever felt the least strange there. Rather he was like a man 'at home' in his new house, accepting naturally his office of host. I do not think any of us could forget his concern for everyone's comfort. Apart from his brief experience of provincial rehearsals he of course realized that actors must keep different hours from other people. But, as much as other people, if not more abundantly, actors must, he clearly felt, need to *be fed*. In this respect, as in so many others, the French might have a more explicitly organized plan of existence, at least in the so explicitly organized Maison de Molière. As for the hours *we* kept, they pained and astonished him. When did we have luncheon? Some of us had breakfasted at eight. By two p.m. he thought only our pathetically stout hearts prevented our fainting there on the stage from sheer inanition. When *did* we eat? Those like myself who played at night and had to make up, dress, and be on the stage at eight o'clock — we hadn't lunched and we couldn't dine!

Before the more protracted last rehearsals ended, Mr. James had invoked his cook and his butler. Somewhere, off-stage, there used to appear a large hamper of delicacies, to which with some ceremony Mr. James would conduct us in

53

two's or three's, as we happened also to be 'off.'
He himself, sandwich in hand, would return to
the fray with obvious relief and satisfaction, leaving us to make our more serious inroads. No other
playwright in my tolerably wide experience ever
thought of feeding his company! At this late hour
I say my grace in memory of those admirable
meals.

They were to be crowned by a supper to which
he invited Mr. and Mrs. Hugh Bell, who were
coming all the way from Yorkshire for the première of 'The American.'

## X

*Reform Club,*
*Pall Mall, S.W.*
Tuesday
[Sept. 22, 1891]

Dear Mrs. Bell.

I am overwhelmed by the magnanimous heroism
of what you are doing for such a fleeting moment —
and to make that moment more divine — greatly
hope you both won't be too exhausted or disconcerted to come and sup with me chez moi (it's
awfully far, I know) — after the play, on Saturday
night —say at *12!* I'm only expecting the Comptons,
Miss Robins and 2 or 3 others — and we shall be
utterly en famille and en pantouffles. It seems terrible not to be able to do more to refresh and reward

such fine practical good friends as you both show yourselves to him qui vous le rend bien, par exemple

Henry James

It is curious on looking back to find that Mr. James's 'American' held the stage too long to meet either the expectation or the convenience of two of the regular London managers. Mr. Charles Wyndham wrote more than once to berate me for obstructing his plans by my failure to tell him when the run of 'The American' was likely to end. Though the play he wanted me for [an adaptation of Dumas's 'Le Demi-Monde' called 'The Fringe of Society'] was to be a 'big production,' requiring, in his opinion, a great deal of preparation, the translation was not yet finished. So between my two engagements there was every reasonable prospect of an interval. The use that should be made of it seemed a question of pressing importance to the Joint Management, even while one of us was struggling to play Mr. James's 'Claire' during an attack of influenza. For the other partner was pledged to a different sort of engagement, unless she could urge prior professional claims. Marion Lea and I were consciously running a race against time.

'Denise' still eluded us. Mr. James had nothing ready of his own. I wrote to Mr. Archer late in October: 'Mr. James is hunting for a play and is very sympathetic over our disappointment. But I seem to have lost faith in our finding a play [in time]. Mitchell says if we don't get something in a few days the marriage [his to Marion Lea] will take place about the end of November. Then

55

comes an interval of honeymooning — then the pantomime and Christmas diversions, then Wyndham's play to be rehearsed, etc., and the "Joint Management" will have had its day and ceased to be.'

As it turned out, while 'The American' was still running (eleven days before the date of Mr. James's next note) Marion Lea had become Mrs. Langdon Mitchell.

She had written me the night before her wedding to reproach me for not sending news about our Shakespeare plan and to assure me, all over again, that marriage was 'to make no difference. Whatever else failed us, we would do 'Twelfth Night' in the Elizabethan fashion, and as for modern stuff, the most modern shone before us in the high light of 'the next Ibsen' — our greatest hope and our greatest anxiety. For there were other bidders in the field. If Mr. Heinemann could secure the play our chances were good.

A day or two after Marion Lea's marriage, Mr. Heinemann was composing for me a letter to Dr. Henrik Ibsen couched in the most persuasive German — a letter in which I urged Mr. Heinemann's claims on the verehrte Meister.

Meanwhile our impatient 'supporters'! — would they weary and drop us out of their calculations? Some such question Mr. James had to meet.

## XI

34 *De Vere Gardens, W.*

November 20th, [1891]

Dear Miss Robins

I have sent your note on — it was all right — in a very cordial one of my own.

Your other note — to me — makes me laugh and almost cry. Trust me, dear Miss Robins, not to 'banish' you! You shall *never* be exiled from my aspirations or calculations; it is, in fact, largely around you that they crystallize. I echo heartily your idea of what we may do together — heartily and gratefully; and it's I who want to appeal to *you* not to doubt — not judge prematurely — only to give me a few months more. Ah me, I wish you were old enough to play Mrs. Vibert! I pray hourly for your rapid healing and am yours always

Henry James

Of productions of Mr. James's four plays 'The American,' 'Guy Domville,' The High Bid,' and 'The Saloon' (in one act), the first had the longest run — in London about two months, Mr. Lubbock says, apart from its record in the provinces.

Not long after that final curtain fell, Mr. James was called to the funeral of Wolcott Balestier. He wrote from the Europäescher Hof, Dresden, a note given here for sake of its postscript.

# XII

Dec. 11th, '91

... Many thanks for your little word of sympathy,
which fell in well with our dreary journey. We got
here Wednesday night — and we stood beside poor
Balestier's grave yesterday — I mean we were in time
for his burial. It is all over — and it is all dismal:
save Dresden itself — which is mild and bright and
picturesque ... I am only resting now — I was dead
with fatigue — but I come home as soon as I at all
easily can — and shall very quickly come to see you.
Thank you again for thinking of me. Dear Wolcott
Balestier is really a quite hideous loss.

Yours always

Henry James

P.S.   I hope meanwhile Twelfth Night is beginning
to mean Twelve times Twelve.

The postscript stands for Mr. James's remembering (even at such a moment!) and sending his
blessing to the particular theatrical project then
in the foreground.

Of the couple of dozen Press notices that have
survived, one of them runs

'The two young American manageresses, Miss
E. Robins and Miss Marion Lea, who produced
"Hedda Gabler" last season, have on foot a project
which is exciting a great deal of interest. It is to
produce "Twelfth Night" on Twelfth Night, in
strictly Elizabethan style, with restored text, little

58

or no scenic effect beyond arras hangings, but with rich costumes and special attention to the music.'

Some of the reasons for this move, which we no doubt laid before Mr. James, are perhaps best conveyed by Marion Lea in one of her letters to me:

'I am distressed by the feeling that our plans which promised so brightly for us both, are going to ground. No matter, dear girl, how fine your parts with Wyndham may be you will never, out of an engagement UNDER any manager, get the advance or the enjoyment which you will do from work fresh from your own hand — and mind. If we do "Twelfth Night" it should be paragraphed as soon as possible — let the announcement of its production in the Temple come as the salt to the dish we serve up; we can wait to announce that. But if you and I are to keep our word to the public of doing work together and following up "Hedda" with other plays, we must give some earnest of that statement's having been in sincerity, and we must give it soon.

I feel that there is such a big future in store for both of us apart from other work we may do, IF WE HOLD TOGETHER, I feel so sure that our combined success will assist our separate success that I should most bitterly regret anything's coming in the way of our immediate progress.'

Mr. James's hope that 'Twelfth Night' is beginning to mean 'Twelve times Twelve' represents faintly the active consideration he had given the matter. Three weeks or so before he posted his message from Dresden, he had written to the Lord Chief Justice invoking his indulgence for our proposal and asking his intervention with the Benchers of the Middle Temple. Lord Coleridge's reply sent our hopes soaring:

*Sussex Square,*
*Hyde Park, W.*
23rd November, 1891

Dear Madam.

I have received your very interesting communication together with letters from Mrs. Henry Pollock and Mr. Henry James. My own tenure of the office of Treasurer of the Middle Temple is just expiring. My successor has been actually elected and he enters on his office on the 10th of December. I learnt from him on Saturday evening that you had already written to him as it was only right you should; but I have undertaken to bring the matter under the consideration of the Bench of the Middle Temple on the 10th of December when we have a meeting to instal Lord Justice Lindley in the Treasurer's Chair. I will see that your wish is fully and favourably considered; but it is a matter on which it is impossible to foresee what view the Bench may take; and beyond undertaking to secure for you a friendly hearing I am afraid I am unable to go.

Believe me to be
dear Madam
Your faithful servant
Coleridge

Miss Elizabeth Robins.


Unfortunately, the Press concerned itself in too lively a fashion with our scheme.

'Miss Elizabeth Robins and Miss Marion Lea have been granted the use of the magnificent hall of the Middle Temple for a performance of "Twelfth Night." In the history of the Middle Temple it is recorded that this hall is the only edifice now standing in which a play of Shakepeare was acted in the poet's lifetime. The play was "Twelfth Night," and was recited before Queen Elizabeth on February 2, 1601.'

This was, to say the least, premature, but we had no idea that our not being responsible for the indiscretion would avail us so little. We learned privately of the very natural resentment on the part of Benchers who perhaps knew nothing about the matter till they read in the papers that they had sanctioned it. Before we could do more than offer our profuse apologies (through our friends and spokesmen, Sir Frederick Pollock, Mr. Cock, Q.C., and Mr. Justice Jeune) — the newspapers had further embroiled us. The horror and misery of the two innocents may be imagined on their reading:

'... The worthy benchers must now expect to be inundated with applications from pretty professionals anxious to secure cheap and dignified pitches for their entertainments. This is perhaps what the old gentlemen in question desire.'

Always Marion Lea and I believed that, if the Press had taken less interest in our hopes, they would have been realized. As it was, 'the old gentlemen' of the Temple as good as told us to run away and play somewhere else.

But this one of the many Joint Management plans may be worth recalling if only that

61

'... other little children
Shall bring our boats ashore'

— and may they hear a voice as heartening as Mr.
James's, with his 'Twelve times Twelve'!

## CHAPTER III

# THE LEADING LADY
# IN LEADING STRINGS

For some weeks, pending my rehearsals in Wyndham's new play for the Criterion, I was in France. From Paris, early in 1892, I wrote Mr. James that I had been seeing 'Hedda Gabler' and looked forward to hearing what he would have to say about the necessity of preceding the performance by 'une conférence par M. Jules Lemaitre' in the hope of making 'Hedda' intelligible to the so-discriminating French public!

Mrs. Vibert was the principal part in Mr. James's new play.

## XIII

34 *De Vere Gardens, W.*
January 4th. [1892]

My dear Miss Robins.

How delightful and inspiring your note. I have lately thought much of you and hoped much for you — *how* much it will be charming to have a chance to tell you on one of the days you are so good as to let me choose. Would either Friday or Saturday afternoon of this week suit you? I shall be delighted to arrive arm in arm with Mrs. Vibert, and in this case should venture to propose my arrival for *4*, as we ought to have a little margin. I am eager for your Paris impressions — am so glad you went. But I delay inquiries — and prepare (myself, not you,) for revelations. Let me add that if neither of the days I mention are right, Thursday would suit me — ah, no it wouldn't — I just, alas, remember! In that case *Wednesday* would: earlyish.

Yours most truly

Henry James

## XIV

*The Reform Club.*

Monday.

Dear Miss Robins.

Your kind note consoles me for a part of the little scare that I had last evening on hearing from you of the other play. I say for a 'part' of it, because only a fraction survived till morning. My fright was mild — and now I don't care. Things must take their chances, whatever they may be — and if one's play isn't good enough to brave accidents it isn't good enough for anything. Besides, honestly speaking, I *didn't* think, from what you told me of it, that the other piece *sounded* dangerous — or sufficiently similar. It didn't even sound to me *really* like a play — but of course I know too little about it. We shall know more in plenty of time. Be easy about your communicative tendency under my uncanny spell. I don't do it on purpose — but I confess I rejoice in the effect.

I had a very long but interesting swim home after leaving you — with what you had told me to think peacefully over as the weary hansom crawled. I wish all the same my production could be produced — and *you* were not so young! At this rate however perhaps you will still play Mrs Vibert — *if* you will. I will wait till next week to knock at your door but then I will knock loud.

Yours always<br>Henry James.

The following notes cannot be read without remorse at the spectacle of incorruptible good manners warring with consternation.

That Mr. James, of all men, should see his own work interrupted by a messenger who hasn't the decency to leave a sealed envelope and go his ways, a messenger who waits (!) for advice about a difficulty which, as Mr. James distractedly writes, '*has* its complicated side' — that he should know the peace of De Vere Gardens had been invaded in the Master's absence to the end that he might cast out devils! — casts, at least, a somewhat chequered light on those early days of '92.

The reference in the next letter to 'Mrs. Bell's version' is of a play, from the Swedish of Alfhild

Agrell, which we renamed 'Karen,' and produced the following May.

## XV

*34 De Vere Gardens, W.*
Tuesday 12th [Jan. '92.]

Dear Miss Robins.

I don't indeed know that while the messenger waits I *can* give you any help about the matter — which *has* its complicated side. The only thing is to present your case frankly to Wyndham — in whose excellent translation I don't believe! — and to write immediately to Mrs Bell as to how the case stands. If Wyndham won't give up his version for hers, you can't be expected to forswear your chance of playing the part because you can't *use* hers. I should think the solution would be in a compromise — your using Mrs Bell's version for those passages that *she* renders best and the other — which will be sure to have badnesses — for such points as *it* may have — Wyndham paying Mrs B. £50 — or more if he will — as a compensation.

In awful haste
Ever yours
H. James

Better.

## XVI

34 De Vere Gardens, W.<br>
Tuesday. [March 22]

Dear Miss Robins.

I am delighted to know I helped you a little. That is I hope you will be able to find that I *have* helped you. I wish indeed I had happened to be at home — or my servant had — for he knew — to exorcise your 7 devils.

I *yearn* for another dramatic evening — with a couple of acts under my arm. Would one of the 1st days of next week suit you? (I have an idea you are always away on Saturday — and *until* this Saturday I am rather taken up.) Would Monday, Tuesday or Wednesday 28th, 29th or 30th do? I hope I am right in supposing that you don't begin at the Criterion *next* week. I yearn still more to hear all about *that,* and am yours always

Henry James

I have always believed there was nothing in any one's experience at all like going to French and Italian plays with Henry James. One of my earliest opportunities in this direction was threatened by an engagement with Mrs. Hugh Bell.

## XVII

May 26th, 1892

Dear Mrs Bell.

I *couldn't*, alas, come in yesterday — I was 'that driven'. I am that driven, at this moment, that I can only thank you very kindly for your note and your gracious relinquishment of the tragic muse. She writes me that she has 'squared' you and *can* go to Sarah with me on Monday.

Your square-ability is more than algebraic, or geometrical, — it is magnanimous. I am pressed — please consider your hand respectfully so. I am impatient for Monday. I was only impatient *at* Tuesday. See to what dregs my intellect is reduced by confusion and believe me

Always yours

Henry James

The next letter refers to the difficulty that had arisen between Mr. Charles Wyndham and myself. He had been paying me a retaining fee for some time, during which I had felt surprise but no misgiving at his casual treatment of the question of formal contract. The terms had been well considered and cordially agreed to with exception of one clause. This dealt with the possibility of Mr. Wyndham's wanting me to continue after the London run, to play the same part in the English provinces (which I did not at all desire, but agreed to) and further that I should accompany him to America if he decided to play a season there. This last I refused.

Later when I ventured to say something about signing our agreement, he again brought up the question of going to America, and as to this I sent him in October what he called my 'ultimatum,' and what I regarded as terminating our association. In November he wrote that though he had begun to negotiate with some other actress, he had been able to allow the matter to stand in abeyance. Now, he could no longer do so. It must be settled in twenty-four hours. Would I come and have a talk? His next communication was by telegram:

> 'Dear Shadow-hunter will try to meet your views if nothing serious prevents.'

Supposing nothing less than that he *had* met my views, the matter rested there — while we worked with might and main at the play — till, during an interval in one of the dress rehearsals, he called me into his private room. On the writing-table lay the agreement I had rejected, with its final paragraph:

> The said Elizabeth Robins also agrees that her services during the period of her engagement shall belong exclusively and absolutely to the said Charles Wyndham whenever and wherever the same may be required.
>
> As Witness the hands of the parties.

Some of my dismay at being given 'till this time to-morrow,' in which 'to take it or leave it,' I shared with Mr. James.

69

## XVIII

Dear Miss Robins.

I am a good deal haunted by what you told me last night in respect to your needful decision of to-day; and yet conscious of the unwisdom — almost the cruelty — of saying anything to you which must of necessity rather worry than guide. *I* can't guide — because I can't offer or guarantee — I can't speak with responsibility, and I am well aware that there are grounds appreciable by yourself alone which must count largely in your determination. Therefore I only want to go to the utmost limit of discretion in saying that you will have all my sympathy in making whatever choice seems to you *on the whole* best, and my friendliest good wishes after the choice is made; but that — I feel as if I ought to write this in very small characters — I shall breathe a silent prayer, while the mystic process goes forward, that you *may* not, by your election, be carried out of the current in which it will be open to me to dream that I shall still be able to do something — to do much — for you. The purpose I entertain of doing work of which the 'American', even on the friendliest view of it, gives no foretaste, has only gathered strength from the events of the last few days — a strength as of welded gold and adamant; and I can't help just murmuring that the way will seem to me all the

70

clearer if in such future contingencies I am not obliged to think of you as *permanently* tied — that is permanently inaccessible. These hurried words are simply that murmur — and they will, I fear, bother you more than assist. But don't think them idle or impertinent — only believe that they represent a great desire to assist you in *any* situation that your decision may lead to.

Yours most truly,<br>Henry James

I did not sign the agreement. Mr. Wyndham telegraphed to Nice for Mrs. Langtry to come and play my part. 'The Fringe of Society' was roundly hissed on the first night, taken off after probably the briefest run in Wyndham's wide experience and consigned to oblivion. No fate so kind was accorded to my 'lack of dependability' and 'utter unreasonableness.' But I had yet to learn the solidarity of Managerial Trade Unionism.

A month later, on May 10th, the Lea-Robins Joint management produced with success Mrs. Hugh Bell's brilliant translation 'Karen.' It was preceded by de Musset's one-act comedy, 'Une Caprice,' in which Marion Lea scored handsomely. But this was naturally not enough to keep her in heart. The next 'Ibsen' seemed as far away as it had been a year before. Exactly as far away if, as they were saying, the verehrto Meister took two years to work his magic. The more immediate plans of the Joint Management hung fire — they did worse. That bright, far-ranging dream! — it shrank and faded, to be, in some small measure, revived later, in the brief activity of the New Century Theatre. Mr. and Mrs. Langdon Mitchell sailed for America at the end of July, 1892, to await, at home, the birth of their child.

In October Mr. James wrote from Brighton to Mrs. Hugh Bell of his further contact with Ibsen. It was to be regretted, for his sake, that Mr. James never saw that magnificent and epoch-making performance, Janet Achurch's original Nora. Janet Achurch was Mrs. Charles Charrington.

## XIX

*Metropole, Brighton*
Oct. 6th, 1892

Dear Mrs Bell.

I gave Bell some assurance (on Tuesday at a London Club,) that I would send you a winged word anent my impression of the little Ibsen-Brighton mixture — the curious Achurch-Robins amalgam — and these few lines are to save my reputation for veracity. They can't do much more — for alas (that is the evidence of last night — the D.'s H.) * the enterprise was born under the evil stars of flatness and feebleness. The Achurches (it sounds like bad grammar,) are of a badness and dreariness so désespèrant that our admirable friend, charming and interesting as she is as the melancholy Linden, has no picture to fit into — no ensemble to compose

* Doll's House.

with — remains a lonely, stranded figure, ploughing through Charringtonian sands. Then she was cursed with a Krogstad so atrocious that he completely took all colour and climax out of her fine scene with him at the beginning of the 3rd Act. Nevertheless she was the one spot of consolation. The houses are good and quiet and dull — this last to match the performance; for a more woeful slowness and sleepiness — like the casual murmurs of incoherent dreams — than the fearsome Charringtons manage to achieve, between them, in their scenes together, is not to be said or sung. Miss Elizabeth bears up bravely, however, and will, I heartily hope, give the affair a gallant coup d'épaule to-night in Hedda. I will try to write a word about this performance tomorrow....

## XX

*Metropole, Brighton.*
Friday, Oct. 7, 1892

Dear Mrs Bell.

A word to let you know how vastly better *Hedda* went off last night than the desolate *D.H.* Everyone was better — Miss R. — for the occasion — not the best that I have ever seen her (she will rise greatly to-night) but very interesting and fine,— and burning the baby, as it were, *more* effectively than ever. Miss Achurch was so much better in the 1st act than at any moment of the D.H. that one hoped a real

73

*coup* for her — but she went to pieces swiftly in lemon-coloured satin (!!!) and staginess, and regurgitated and ranted till you couldn't believe it. She makes a loud, showy, belle-femme, Medusa-Thea. The fellow (if I may be allowed the expression) who did Krogstad so badly (Julian Cross), was *excellent* as Brack — and little Thalberg made an extremely creditable Tesman. Poor Charrington, as Lövborg, was the stumbling-block — he had taken an overdose of morphia (MORPHIA) for neuralgia and went thro' it somnambulistically sick. His wife was in anguish (she had given him the dose!) and this was doubtless partly why she was so nervous and tragic.

Miss Elizabeth gave us — the Achurches, Archers and me — a charming little supper afterwards at the Bedford. The house was excellent. I catch a train.

Yours ever,
Henry James

## XXI

34, *De V. Gdns.*
Oct. 10, '92

[To Mrs. Hugh Bell]

. . . .

I am glad my account of Brighton didn't seem too grey. Miss Elizabeth will probably by this time have illuminated you further — and I hope she will have felt able to say to you that whatever the week may have done for the Charringtons it did, palpably, something for Hedda-Linda (or whatever the lone widow's name was.)

To the mind of a friendly spectator in the stalls it did *this* — that it broke for the hour the damnable spell of her NOT acting. It was a comfort, from this point of view, to see her simply doing her work and plying her trade. I echo heartily your view of her 'unworldly careering' — and feel like Betsy Trotwood (wasn't it?) with her 'Let us have no meandering'. Let us, at all events, have no unworldly careering. She ought to take more what she can get — to do whenever she can, *any*thing she can — be it Norwegian or not. Too little, alas, however, comes in her way — and she is, after all, indifferent (so it seems to me.) This quite in your single ear — I don't mean that you have only one; or that the other is the only married. . . .

Henry James

## CHAPTER IV

# 'FROM BEWILDERMENT
# TO MADNESS'

The 'news was about a play destined to be heard more of later. It was called in its Swedish short story form, 'Befriad,' called in the English stage form, 'Alan's Wife' and called by Mr. James (before he had heard it read) 'the dramatic gem.' This description represents only the reflection of my personal enthusiasm. He would not in his most ironic mood have applied such a description to that terrific little play, which I believe filled him with horror.

This letter also points to the fact that, more than a year after the London production of 'The American,' Mr. James's play was running in the provinces, and that he was still concerned with it to the extent of writing a new fourth act.

'The Norse grammar' was his contribution towards strengthening the meagre equipment that had already helped me to read Ibsen in the original, and to translate, on commission, some of Björnson's fiction.

The 'great news,' not yet available, referred of course to the long and eagerly expected 'next Ibsen.'

76

# XXII

34 *De Vere Gardens, W.*
Monday, Nov. 7th, [1892]

Dear Miss Robins.

Your news — though not the *great* news — is of a palpitating interest and I shall be delighted to have more of it. I will come on Wednesday (next) with pleasure for this purpose and should rather prefer the evening, (after dinner) if that is equally convenient to yourself. I will turn up on the said Wednesday at 9 if I hear nothing from you to the contrary. I congratulate you with all my heart on the acquisition of the dramatic gem. *Surely* you must make it twinkle before me. I will think my best on the subject of the little play in verse — but nothing occurs to me off-hand. Delicate one-act English plays haven't, so far as I know, the ghost of an existence. Thanks for your inquiries about the new 4th act of 'The American.' Yes — it is finished, but some of [the] alterations (slight but indispensable) in the previous parts, to fit it, are not. I go on the 14th, however, to Bath, to make over the whole and my views and ideas on it, to the eager interpreters. It will (the new act — of comedy!!) be played for the first time on the 18th, at Bristol; but I probably shall not see it till Friday, December 9th at *Croydon.* Will you (Ibsen permitting) come with me to Croydon on that evening to see it? I see there are easy trains back to town after the performance.

Don't trouble to write unless Wednesday evening does *not* suit you. Believe me, yours always,

Henry James

P.S. The Norse grammar goes to you to-day by book-post.

It seemed to be part of Ibsen's mission to set people's nerves quivering, whether with fury or delight. Months before 'The Master Builder' reached these shores the excitement that was set up by mere anticipation, will never be credited in these times, theatrically so calm, if not be-calmed.

One can only say it was different in the '90's, when to despair of Ibsen's coming 'in time' was next door to despair of the highest incentive to work.

The delay did not, perhaps, drive anybody to drink; it was said to have driven one person to marriage. Whether more of the drama inherent in that story of anticipation will ever seem worth telling, a summary is all that need find place here. Impatience for the play to come was exacerbated by the darkness that shrouded it. Who could be sure it would be a woman's play — why not another 'Brand,' or 'Enemy of the People'? It might not be anybody's play. It might not be a book that anybody would want to buy. Alternatively, it might be the chance of a lifetime.

These possibilities were weighed in the state of 'irremediable fever,' that (as Mr. James candidly confessed) could infect even a critic so little predisposed as he — 'that inward strife which is an inevitable heritage of all inquiring contact with the master.' The moment came when the would-be publisher's nerves could not tolerate waiting in England. Mr. William Heinemann went to Norway and came back with the rights virtually in his pocket.

But that was only the beginning. Of the play it was not so much as the beginning. Neither the man who had committed himself to publishing it, nor anybody else had even now the faintest idea what the play would be about. People lived on supposition, and were as hot over it as though they knew what it was they were contending for. They could at least debate: who should be associated in the stage-production? Who would finance it and at what cost? Most pressing of all, in point of time: who should turn it into English? Here, at any hour, would be arriving the first sheets of a play about which only one thing was certain: it must be translated at lightning speed, since the English copyright had to be taken out simultaneously with the Norwegian.

A private agreement that the English dress should come from the hands of two women — Mrs. Hugh Bell and myself — stirred passion to such a pitch, that in deference to the peace of the publisher, we voluntarily abandoned what we could have exacted — abandoned it, that is, so far as any public knowledge of our share was concerned.

All this before the first page of the original had reached England. All this and more. For apart from translators and possible players there were people who showed a curiosity about the new Ibsen unaccountable to those others who still, in print and in private, protested that Ibsen was not only negligible but neglected — 'dead and buried.' They would have been surprised at the liveliness of interest shown among people not only outside the Theatre but well outside the little circle of so-called 'Ibsenites' — people far from sympathetic intellectually towards Ibsen's genius or, like Mr. James, definitely hostile to its form of expression, 'bare,' 'bald,' 'bourgeois.'

Yet not Mr. James alone came up and down those seventy-four steps for news from Norway, but people like Sir Frederick and Lady Pollock, and I am not sure but Sir Frederick's mother, the friend of Macready, Juliet Lady Pollock; Sidney Colvin too, and Oswald Crawfurd; Mr. Cock, Q.C. and his wife; Victoria, Lady Welby; Mr. and Mrs. Moscheles; Mr. Stephen Coleridge, Mrs. W. K. Clifford; Hon. Mrs. Norman Grosvenor; Mr. J. M. Horsburgh, Registrar of the London University; Hon. Mrs. Lyulph Stanley; Mrs. Humphry Ward; W. T. Stead; Gertrude Bell, her father, and presently, her grandfather, Sir Lowthian Bell; Mrs. Cashel Hoey; Miss Geneviève Ward; Mr. William Moore, Classical Master in the Philological School; Rhoda Broughton; Mrs. John Richard Green; Mr. R. B. Haldane; Lady Arabella Romilly . . . and others in addition to those who might naturally be expected to feel some interest in the successor to 'Hedda Gabler' — Bernard Shaw; Beerbohm Tree; Mr. and Mrs. Crackanthorpe and their gifted and lovable son, Hubert; Arthur Symons; Mortimer Menpes; and Oscar Wilde.

Special people, like Mr. James and Mrs. Hugh Bell, knew that by an act of grace towards Mr. Heinemann, the Norwegian publisher was to send

80

(as fast as they were printed off) three pulls of the yet unnamed play; one for Mr. Gosse, one for Mr. Archer, one for me. These ultimately arrived in small, in very small, violently agitating spurts — or as one might say, in volts, projected across the North Sea in a series of electric shocks. The news of their arrival flew from the Strand to Manchester Square Mansions, from there to Yorkshire and to De Vere Gardens — while I sat and hugged my good luck in being able to read the Norwegian instead of waiting on the combined services of Mr. Gosse and Mr. Archer.

The first sheets must have begun to arrive about November 8th. Mrs. Hugh Bell, who was fathoms deep in a very different literary collaboration wrote from Yorkshire on the 9th: 'What, oh what, of Gewirrwiggs?' — the name we rejoiced in giving the play before Ibsen had taught us to say 'The Master Builder.' I was to send her constant bulletins of how the thing went on. Mr. James, being in London, could come himself and so hear more than I had time to write.

## XXIII

34 *De Vere Gardens, W.*

Dear Miss Robins.

Saturday evening will suit me down to the ground — or as I ought in your case to say, up to the skies: and I shall be eager — and not later than *nine*.

Yours ever<br>Henry James

Wednesday.

To Mrs. Hugh Bell (in Yorkshire) I wrote on Nov. 12.

Later

... Third instalment Ibsen play. I am more in a maze than ever! Fine scene between Herdal and Solness with good nervous climax, best thing so far in the play — and at that point another young woman is sprung upon us — but she doesn't smile at me — I'm horribly afraid she's the heroine! So far the acting opportunities are all with Solness and even if he has little else to do — which is inconceivable — he will be fine — fine, fine, but alas, the women! L.[Lisa]

I find I've left all this side unwritten on! I had a cosy chat over the fire with H.J. yesterday. I told him bits and read him bits (I.P.* of course) under seal of secrecy except so far as you're concerned. He will be writing you 'impressions'. I embarked on this much frankness somewhat as a means of getting him away from 'Befriad' which he's itching to hear. He comes Tuesday of next week to hear if the Ibsen heroine has appeared yet and what she's like. He'll faint when he hears! This is her portrait. 'Middle height, supple, (graceful?) delicately built, a little sunburnt, wears a "tourist's dress" (?) with a skirt fastened up (or pinned up), sailor collar turned away from the throat and little sailor hat on her head. Has a knapsack on her back; rug in a shawlstrap and alpenstock!' How I *hate her!!!*

[On outside of envelope:]

Second instalment to-day: More in the dark than ever — think the old man's stark mad.

Nov. 12/92

* Intensely private.

## XXIV

34 *De Vere Gardens, W.*
November 13th.

Dear Miss Robins.

It is all painfully, terribly, interesting! I am fearfully impatient for Tuesday afternoon — and beside myself with curiosity as to who or what the 'other woman' can be. *This* reflection — however — is somewhat lurid — that Kaia, the black silk wife, another other woman, *must* be (in a 3-act play and by the middle of the 1st,) the *only* woman, so that the 'heroine' is, of necessity, one or other of them. Perhaps she *is* the black silk wife. You don't tell me whether the other woman is the wife of the 'young couple'. Nor whether the thunder-roll from the *other* translator (on receipt of emendations), has yet come back to you. These things, however, I must curb myself to wait for till Tuesday at 5. — I really think you must, if possible, come to Croydon on the 9th; for I've just got back my type-copy of my new act from the copyist and am struck with its being — heaven forgive me! — very good! The following week is *Aldershot* — but the trains make it impossible — none back to town after 8.30.

Yours always,
Henry James

On that same day, Nov. 13, Mrs. Hugh Bell was writing to me from Yorkshire:

'I am frantically interested . . . I wonder if by the end of this Act you will be able to tell? [Whether the new Ibsen was going to "do" for me] I don't like your young tourist, but after all she may be called upon to do all sorts of splendid things — but I shall be disappointed if she isn't a villain! In the meantime I feel that by this day week the question will be settled one way or the other, this question that has been a part of one's life since the summer . . . write, write to me.

P.S. I wonder what H.J. thought.'

On Nov. 15th I wrote to Mrs. Hugh Bell after 'a long visit from H.J.' and told her what I thought he thought; also that 'W.H. [William Heinemann] comes, now, in a few minutes and will be "frantic" as his "express" letter puts it, to have bits read to him, so I can't post it off to you . . . just yet. W. A. [William Archer] as well as the rest is a good deal puzzled; but he says the 1st Act is powerful and fascinating though he can't "see it" on the English stage. I am desolate. James cries, hold! and tries to make me think I could get a lot out of Hilda, but in his heart he knows I'm not the one to play Hilda.'

Nov. 16th?

'. . . W.A. seems less hopeful since the second instalment of the 2nd Act. He writes: "the interest certainly hangs fire," &c., &c. *I* fear the thing is hopeless! — but I did not say as much to W.H. last night — for until the whole thing is here, it's absurd to say anything definite. How thankful I am I did not let H. say in print that I was going to produce it. . . . I don't know what to do, or look forward to, now this Ibsen bubble bids fair to burst.'

84

# XXV

Dear Mrs Bell.

I have meant to tell you, for some days past, something (in response to your last inspiring invitation,) about the interest, the really *sore* intensity of the situation here; but I have waited just *because* it was interesting and the day-to-day turn of affairs seemed to promise the really *definite* — which, however, still eludes the tormented spirit. Of all contingencies — as almost always happens — the *least* expected appears to be the one which is en train to take place: the precious play has, at last, for some days past, been arriving piecemeal — in tormentingly small bits of proof — up to (yesterday) the 1st 3rd or quarter of the 2nd Act (the acts are long, evidently,) only to demonstrate — so far as can *yet* be judged — that it is after all disconcerting and disappointing. Voilà le grant mot lâché — it is a question, I surmise, at *present,* of whether it will do at all at *all,* as they say in Ireland. (All this of course is *intensely* private and confidential.) I have been kindly favoured with the communication of most of it, and am utterly bewildered and mystified. It is like an uncanny trick of the hard and shrewd old Norseman, safe in his far-off Christiania with his splendid bargain. That at least is what it *looks* like as yet — of course it's too soon to be wholly sure.

But this *week* — the next 2 or 3 days — will settle the awful doubt. There are but 3 acts — so they *must*. It is all most strange, most curious, most vague, most horrid, most 'middle-classy' in the peculiar ugly Ibsen sense — and alas most *un*promising for Miss Elizabeth or for any *woman*. What is already clear is that a *man* is the central figure — the Hedda, and the women quite subordinate; and the man, alas an elderly, whitehaired architect, or Baumeister, is although a strange and interesting, a fearfully *charmless,* creature. It doesn't as yet *begin* to shape itself as a play, an action — but only as an obscure and Ibseny tale, or psychological picture, requiring infinite elucidation. There are 3 women; an old wife, an anæmic girl, a young female accountant, with a green shade over her eyes — and most unexpectedly Hilda Wangel — out of the 'Lady from the Sea' (do you remember her?) back again as a pert and strong-minded female pedestrian tourist, with a sailor hat, a short frock, a knapsack (full of 'clothes for the wash') and the coquetry of the celebrated Peckham — par même of Redcar! Do you see Miss Elizabeth in that galère? Hilda will evidently come out, greatly, in the next acts, but she will come out further and further from Miss E. And the fact remains that the quinquigenarian architect *must* be the heroine — Miss Elizabeth must do *him*. Seriously it is, as yet, all deception — though interesting in itself. Miss E. is very low — but she has prob-

86

ably written you as I have. Moreover there is a *chance* yet, and Ci vuol pazienza.

I am to learn more to-morrow and I will write you again. Ce vieux farceur! Heinemann is *already* banging at the door for a decision — and Archer and Gosse are exchanging cartels! Don't you see them all? — ever jusqu'à yours, dear Mrs Bell, most under the rosely.

Henry James

## XXVI

34 *De Vere Gardens, W.*
Nov. 18th [1892]

Dear Miss Robins.

I was unable to send you my sympathy last night; but it goes to-day, very heartily — with lots of disappointment, too, at the loss of the intenser light I was hoping for. I am beset by the feeling that it is the damned old Norseman — the plundering pirate and Berserker, that has made you ill, and that if you caught a cold it was from the terrible moral draught in which you have been living and which blows straight across from Ibsen to Heinemann. I am so taken every hour of the next 3 or 4 days, that I don't know *when* to beg you for a scrap of time in which you can tell me *what* turn, in heaven's name the dark drama is taking. I go to Oxford — till night — to-morrow afternoon; and am in a fearful embroilment on Sunday. I think I shall try and knock at

87

your door to *ask* — late this afternoon — I am dining out. But I hope with all my heart you are better — even if the play *isn't*. If you give me, at your convalescent convenience, a line, suggesting some hour, you would infinitely gratify yours most faithfully

Henry James

## XXVII

Dear Miss Robins.

I languish to know if anything has happened — and if so what? I know that if it has you are up to your neck in preoccupations and yet I boldly inquire: *Did* your possible accomplice read the full play — and did he cool off, or (infinitely more probably) freeze on? Is it finished and when can a fellow see it? I sit in darkness — and long for light. I feel as if the most interesting things were going on behind a closed door. *When* could you open it — 'on a crack' — for

Yours most particularly

Henry James?

Dec. 9th. [1892]

One manager after another had been offered the chance to godfather the new Ibsen. In my conviction that one of the established theatres should, and would, give 'The Master Builder' a production worthy of it, I had found myself mistaken.

## XXVIII

Dear Miss Robins.

There's a lot I *want* to 'answer' in your most interesting but most melancholy letter of Sunday; but I *wait,* because I am infinitely pressed with occupation and I know you are; and because 2nd, I further know that I shall meet you to-morrow at Mrs Green's when I heartily hope that we shall be able to take an hour — of appointment — for the rest of the ineffable Ibsen. Meanwhile I am

Yours always

Henry James

In the thick of the Ibsen councils I turned to my countryman for guidance as to English customs in polite correspondence.

## XXIX

34 *De Vere Gardens, **W***.
Tuesday p.m. [Dec. 13, '92]
Dear Miss Robins.

'Dear Lady Arabella Romilly' if you know her only *just* — and are writing for the first time; 'dear Lady Arabella', if you are writing for the second; and 'The Lady A.' precisely, on the outside. — I scrawled you three words this a.m. — and hope you are really to be present to-morrow at Mrs G.'s anticipated dinner. Bravo Ibsen! If the end is as you say it will be magnificent — and utterly incomprehensible in the Strand.

You must tell me more.

Yours ever

Henry James

As indicated in Mr. James's previous letter, [xxix] the ending of 'The Master Builder,' had shed a light by which I could see with growing clearness that this, of all plays in the world, was, after all, my play.

How, where, with whom, it should be acted, I had not the faintest idea till mid-December brought an unexpected enthusiast for the great part of Solness.

My last interchange with Mr. James in '92 before I went to Yorkshire for the holidays, seems to have followed a visit from him on December 19th, during which I doubtless told him what I wrote the next day to Mrs. Hugh Bell: that I had read 'The Master Builder' to the Manager of the Haymarket and that he (Tree) was 'swept away by Solness, wants to play it . . . H.J. was here yesterday — he's a dear. He's coming out to Weybridge to walk on the heath with me — proposed it himself' — I say proudly.

Mr. Tree had good reasons of his own for not wanting at the moment to produce 'The Master Builder' at the Haymarket, and the guardians of that play had reasons for not wanting it ever done there, in view of the amazing alterations demanded by Mr. Tree.

January found Herbert Waring and me looking for another Theatre and another backer. For a moment we hoped we had discovered him — in Mr. Löwenfeldt, then lessee of the Lyric, if I remember.

## XXX

34 *De Vere Gardens, W.*
Dear Miss Robins.

You lead me on from wonder to wonder and from bewilderment to madness. I should think your own reason would totter. It is of course unspeakably thrilling — but wild horses wouldn't drag an *opinion* out of me — any, that is, save this *one,* that before they've all done with you they will have simply, among them, laid you in your grave. Of what do they think and of what leathery strong stuff — the beautiful, *our* beautiful, 'artistic temperament' is made? All this, alas, isn't the great art of acting — and so far it's all damnably wrong. As for everything in the question save your *health* — your survival — I don't see how, in the kaleidoscopic rotation, one particular agglomeration of the pink and blue grass matters more than another. Still — have a theatre if you *can!* — but not beyond the grave — *here,* now, something for us mortals to take hold of. Löwenfeldt *may* be the New Era in Polish Jew form — and Heinemann may be the agent of a divine revelation.

91

For heaven's sake, at any rate, take care of your cold and let me come to see you right soon again.

Yours always<br>Henry James

January 19th. [1892]

On January 20th I had signed an agreement to produce 'The Master Builder.'

## XXXI

34 *De Vere Gardens, W.*

Dear Miss Robins.

Glory, Glory, Hallelujah! Your absence of detail is cruel, but I will come in, with pleasure, to batten on detail on *Tuesday* at 9 p. m. Perturbèd spirit, *REST* — before anything else! I post you off by hand the whole of the kindly-lent, but (save Act I) as yet unread, alas, Ibsen. I have been a brute to keep 2 and 3 so long; but have waited, in a fever of other necessities, for the right hour to gobble him down — which didn't come. I have had to give more hours and instants than I *have,* to some pressing reading for a long article I am writing for a terribly fixed date. However, I suppose the purchaseable book is now due from one day to the other. I *can* now, perhaps — almost — buy a book of Heinemann's!

Till Tuesday. Yours always<br>Henry James

January 22nd. [1893]

## CHAPTER V

# THE MASTER BUILDER

Before the next letter was written he had published in the *Pall Mall Gazette* an article:

## IBSEN'S NEW PLAY

### BY HENRY JAMES

In spite of its having been announced in many quarters that Ibsen would never do, we are still to have another chance, which may indeed very well not be the last, of judging of the question for ourselves. Not only has the battered Norseman, in the evening of his career, had the energy to fling yet again into the arena one of those bones of contention of which he has in an unequalled degree the secret of possessing himself, but practised London hands have been able to catch the mystic missile in its passage and are on the point of flourishing it, as they have flourished others, before our eyes. The English version of 'Bygmester Solness,' lately prepared by Mr. Edmund Gosse and Mr. William Archer and now, under the title of 'The Master-Builder,' about to appear as a volume, is, on Monday afternoon next and on the following afternoons, to be presented at the

93

Trafalgar Square Theatre by a company of which Mr. Herbert Waring, Miss Elizabeth Robins, and Miss Louise Moodie are the principal members. In addition to an opportunity of reading the play I have had the pleasure of seeing a rehearsal of the performance — so that I already feel something of the responsibility of that inward strife which is an inevitable heritage of all inquiring contact with the master. It is perhaps a consequence of this irremediable fever that one should recklessly court the further responsibility attached to uttering an impression into which the premature may partly enter. But it is impossible, in any encounter with Ibsen, to resist the influence of at least the one kind of interest that he exerts at the very outset, and to which at the present hour it may well be a point of honour promptly to confess one's subjection. This immediate kind is the general interest we owe to the refreshing circumstance that he at any rate gives us the sense of life, and the practical effect of which is ever to work a more or less irritating spell. The other kind is the interest of the particular production, a varying quantity and an agreeable source of suspense — a happy occasion, in short, for that play of intelligence, that acuteness of response, whether in assent or in protest, which it is the privilege of the clinging theatre-goer to look forward to as a result of the ingenious dramatist's appeal, and his sad predicament for the most part to miss yet another and another chance to achieve. With Ibsen (and that is the exceptional joy, the bribe to rapid submission) we can always count upon the chance. Our languid pulses quicken as we begin to note the particular direction taken by the attack on a curiosity inhabiting by way of a change the neglected region of the brain.

In 'The Master-Builder' this emotion is not only kindled very early in the piece — it avails itself to the full of the right that Ibsen always so liberally concedes it of being still lively after the piece is over. His independence, his perversity, his intensity, his vividness, the hard compulsion of his strangely inscrutable art, are present in full measure, together with that quality which comes almost uppermost when it is a question of seeing him on the stage, his peculiar blessedness to actors. *Their* reasons for liking him it would not be easy to overstate; and surely, if the public should ever completely renounce him, players enamoured of their art will still be found ready to interpret him for that art's sake to empty benches. No dramatist of our time has had more the secret, and has kept it better, of making their work interesting to them. The subtlety with which he puts them into relation to it eludes analysis, but operates none the less strongly as an incitement. Does it reside mainly in the way he takes hold of their imagination, or in some special affinity with their technical sense; in what he gives them or in what he leaves it to them to give; in the touches by which the moral nature of the character opens out a vista for them; or in the simple fact of connection with such a vivified whole? These are questions at any rate that Mr. Herbert Waring, Miss Robins, Miss Moodie, enviable with their several problems, doubtless freely ask themselves, or even each other, while the interest and the mystery of 'The Master-Builder' fold them more and more closely in.

What is incontestable is the excitement, the amusement, the inspiration of dealing with material so solid and so fresh. The very difficulty of it makes a common cause, as the growing ripeness of preparation makes a common enthusiasm.

I shall not attempt to express the subject of the play more largely than to say that its three acts deal again, as Ibsen is so apt to deal, with the supremely critical hour in the life of an individual, in the history of a soul. The individual is in this case not a Hedda, nor a Nora, nor a Mrs. Alving, nor a Lady from the Sea, but a prosperous architect of Christiania, who, on reaching a robust maturity, encounters his fate all in the opening of a door. This fate — infinitely strange and terrible, as we know before the curtain falls — is foreshadowed in Miss Elizabeth Robins, who, however, in passing the threshold, lets in a great deal more than herself, represents a heroine conceived, as to her effect on the action, with that shameless originality which Ibsen's contemners call wanton and his admirers call fascinating. Hilda Wangel, a young woman whom the author may well be trusted to have made more mystifying than her curiously commonplace name would suggest, is only the indirect form, the animated clock-face, as it were, of Halvard Solness's destiny; but the action, in spite of obscurities and ironies, takes its course by steps none the less irresistible. The mingled reality and symbolism of it all give us an Ibsen within an Ibsen. His subject is always, like the subjects of all first-rate men, primarily an idea; but in this case the idea is as difficult to catch as its presence is impossible to overlook. The whole thing throbs and flushes

96

with it, and yet smiles and mocks at us through it as if in conscious super-subtlety. The action at any rate is superficially simple, more single and confined than that of most of Ibsen's other plays; practically, as it defines itself and rises to a height, it leaves the strange, doomed Solness, and the even stranger apparition of the joyous and importunate girl (the one all memories and hauntings and bondages, the other all health and curiosity and youthful insolence), face to face on unprecedented terms — terms, however, I hasten to add, that by no means prevent the play from being one to which a daughter, as they say in Paris, may properly take her mother. Of all Ibsen's heroines Hilda is indeed perhaps at once the most characteristic of the author and the most void of offence to the 'general.' If she has notes that recall Hedda, she is a Hedda dangerous precisely because she is *not yet blasée* — a Hedda stimulating, fully beneficent in intention; in short, 'reversed,' as I believe the author defined her to his interpreters. From her encounter with Halvard Solness many remarkable things arise, but most of all perhaps the spectators' sense of the opportunity offered by the two rare parts; and in particular of the fruitful occasion (for Solness from beginning to end holds the stage) seized by Mr. Herbert Waring, who has evidently recognized one of those hours that actors sometimes wait long years for — the hour that reveals a talent to itself as well as to its friends and that makes a reputation take a bound. Whatever, besides refreshing them, 'The Master-Builder' does for Ibsen with London playgoers, it will render the service that the curious little Norwegian repertory has almost always ren-

97

dered the performers, even to the subsidiary figures, even to the touching Kaia, the Ragnar, the inevitable Dr. Herdal, and the wasted wife of Solness, so carefully composed by Miss Moodie.


There had been considerable difference of opinion as to the dressing of the girl in 'The Master Builder.' I insisted on following Ibsen's directions. That I was altogether successful in this, I will not go so far as to say. The distance I went greatly disturbed my friends—with a single exception.

Memory has played me false in one detail. I have said elsewhere the first occasion of Mr. James's expressed disapproval was by word of mouth after the rehearsal he attended. This was not so. It was after a talk with Mr. and Mrs. Gosse (who had seen the clothes and were 'much agitated' about them) that Mr. James made by letter his first impassioned appeal that I should mend my ways — yes, mend even Ibsen's ways, in the matter of dress.

## XXXII

34 *De Vere Gardens, W.*
[Feb. 17th midnight]

Dear Miss Robins.

I hear from Mrs. Gosse to-night an alarming — a really pessimistic account of Hilda's dress, as revealed to-day, and am made so uneasy by it (they — she and her husband — are much agitated), that

THE MUSE OF CASTLES IN THE AIR

ELIZABETH ROBINS as HILDA in IBSEN'S "MASTER BUILDER" 1893
...... Theres only one possible dwelling place
for human happiness
........ Castles in the air!   ACT III.

[*Lady Bell's Lettering*]

I can't go to bed without holding up warning and imploring hands. Please don't think me obtrusive or outrageous for doing so — too much depends upon your being absolutely *right* on that question. BE right, I *beseech* you; amend it, improve it, reconstruct it utterly while yet there is time. If everything else is right and your frock is wrong, that wrongness may —*will* — determine the fate of the play. Throw Ibsen's prescriptions to the winds if practically they betray you. There are reasons too imperative for it — and you accept perils enough for him, to have a right to discriminate there. Don't be fantastic — be *pretty*, be agreeable, in the right key. I can't help being sorry you have only one gown; if so it ought to have a very positive felicity. A 1000 eyes will peck at it for 2 and $\frac{1}{2}$ hours. Throw yourself into the dressmaker's arms. Be better, be darker, be longer! And wear something else in Act II. The speech about the 'same dress' doesn't matter — it's *arbitrary*. Forgive me; and DON'T in your frantic haste answer this.

Yours always

Henry James

Those who best understand the stage will take it as another evidence of Mr. James's closeness to the theatrical form, that he should consider with his own peculiar intensity this question of how a part should be dressed. It is a consideration carrying all the weight Mr. James would give it, since not only the fortunes of the player are at stake, but the fortunes of the play and of the whole enterprise. Our difference was not a difference in concern. It is only now on rereading these letters that I see I was mistaken when I said (in an Ibsen Centenary lecture, 1928) it was merely Hilda's collar that Mr. James found fault with. It was merely the collar I tried to improve. The general air of combined utility and negligence, which he deplored, was an effect I aimed at. I cannot imagine how he managed to forgive me for not struggling to comply with his adjuration: 'be pretty, be agreeable.' As to the obnoxious only dress — no whit 'better,' no 'darker,' no 'longer' — the sole change I offered him was the addition of hobnailed boots.

His reference to the newspaper accounts of the first performance has carried me back to such of the notices as are available. It is interesting to find Mr. James, little as he expected from the general run of critics, expecting more from them on this occasion than the actors did. He must have looked in the next morning's Press for something that could only come, and to a great extent did come, later. After all, neither he nor I, not Mr. Archer, nor Mr. Gosse, none of us on our first contact with this particular play, had shown a very ready understanding of it. Partly on that account I have set down our common bewilderment and chagrin, though not the unwilling submission, of one reader of the original, to that haunting poetry of the Norwegian spell.

Mr. Archer, who was not likely to let the other critics off too lightly, wrote in *The Illustrated London News,* on February 25th: 'There can be no doubt that we have made an extraordinary advance in what may, perhaps, be called artistic open-mindedness. Who could have foreseen, five, three, even two years ago, that a play so fantastic in its atmosphere, so recondite in its symbolism, so daring in its technique, as "The Master Builder," would hold an English audience spell-bound and would be received by the Press, not, certainly, with enthusiasm, but with decent courtesy and no more than reasonable indignation?'

It must have been partly Mr. James's sympathy with the actors' efforts and their hopes that made him denounce the daily paper critics so handsomely. For, however baffled or indignant with the play, the critics were astonishingly kind to the actors.

## XXXIII

34 *De Vere Gardens, W.*
Feb. 21st.

Dear Miss Robins.

I meant to have written you a word last night — but from the moment I left the T.S.T. [Trafalgar Square Theatre] till a very late hour I was unceasingly occupied. This morning the odious newspapers make me want still more to do so — and say what I hadn't time for in that hurried greenroom moment. I have looked at the papers and there is little edification in them of course. They are stupid, angry and mean. The weaknesses of the play do indeed come out strongly in representation, but it would have been only honest in them to acknowledge also its *hold,* the odd baffling spell it works and the remarkable spell of the interpretation. I neither hoped nor expected much from the effect of the play as a play — but I am beautifully undisappointed in what I *did* expect — the very great impression you personally produced and the admirable nature of your performance. It enlarges delightfully one's vision of your powers and justifies triumphantly your bold undertaking of the part. The freshness, the brilliancy, the variety, the intelligence and power and charm of your creation there was but one voice yesterday to recognize, as there is but one result of it all for you to look for — the biggest lift to your professional position. You have had in other words a great and delightful success — which was exactly what was to be demonstrated. As I have received as a subscriber a stall for the Independent Theatre * to-night — I shall probably go, and perhaps shall find you there. I shan't see the *M.B.* again to-day, but I expect to to-morrow or at furthest Thursday. — I thought Waring *extremely* good — various and interesting, intelligent and coloured: BUT distinctly not loud enough. You *were* — keep it up, *up,* UP. Miss M. disappointing — entirely too monotonously and conventionally *tragic* — making poor Mrs S. [Solness] a stale theatrical *category,* instead of a special person. The *doll* scene with you, in Act III., is rendered very dangerous by her slow intensity

* For production of Mr. George Moore's play "The Strike at Arlingford."

102

of solemnity. But there is no doubt the play does what one expected it would do — of course it doesn't do what one didn't. It lives and makes its life felt on the consenting. The others were out of the account from the 1st. I see the *Telegraph* and the *Chronicle* have some liberality. But it is 'in theatrical circles' — or with the independent spectator that your own achievement will tell.

Yours always<br>Henry James

## XXXIV

34 De Vere Gardens, W.<br>[Sat. March 4th, 1893]

Dear Mrs Bell.

I saw the prima donna yesterday — went to the dernière at the T.S.T. [Trafalgar Square Theatre], and had a good bit of talk with her. The play, however, is to be promoted — vous le saurez du reste déjà — to the evening bill at the Vaudeville. The house yesterday was *full* — the best (but one) they have had. They are glad of the 'evening bill' &c., but more hopeful (of 2 or 3 weeks of it, of course, only,) than confident. The sad thing is that — il paraît — neither she nor Waring have as yet touched a penny of money. When Heinemann, and the salaries and all the expenses, theatre-rent, staff, 2 managers, &c. &c. are paid, there is nothing for those 2 unhappy 5th wheels to the coach! It is very wretched. Of course the next week or two may make the difference. But the fact that she remains as yet as poor as before singularly diminishes any exuberance of one's own satisfaction. She is apparently as *moderately* sorry as it is given to her remarkableness to be. For the rest — oh a 100 times yes — she has helped herself, *doubled* her position. As for the no-money element, she didn't at any rate renounce money to do it. She says it will, however, practically 'lead to NOTHING!' She will be thought more remarkable, but be just as remarkably let alone. This isn't so, however — she has given herself *more* chances. In talking with her of course one continues to *batter* one's self against that quiet individuality of determination — not to say perversity of it — which takes from me, at least — all sense of effect and fruit from my words. She sees her life in a certain way — and that's the end of it. But she *will,* all the same, I think, arrive. The play went yesterday better, I think, than I had seen it before; but I am singularly tired of it! Watch next week with interest. There is to be, however, no press-night. Excuse the frantic haste, dear Mrs. Bell, of yours always

Henry James

March 4th.

George W. Smalley was, for many years, London correspondent to the *New York Tribune*. His good word carried great weight in America. But for Mr. James this powerful personage would not have written about 'The Master Builder' as he did.

XXXV

34 De Vere Gardens, W.<br>March 4th

Dear Miss Robins.

I have asked Smalley for Tuesday or Wednesday — I will let you know his answer as soon as I get it.

Meanwhile please believe 3 or 4 things.

1° That Hilda *has* increased that indefinite but potent element in the problem your *chances.*

2° That your talent is of the kind that sooner or later arrives as the French say.

3° That you have advantages over almost *every one* else in having an *author* at your complete disposal — who only asks for a little patience and a few months more of margin. He is full of purposes and resolutions — and oh if *he* could only find a valiant and civilized young manager, you would find yourself bettered — I believe — by the same stroke. But this will come. It is only a question of a few more months.

I have *very* great visions and resolutions. Take a share — a 1000 shares in them: you have nothing to pay.

Yours ever<br>Henry James

P.S. I have sent for the book: it goes straight.

105

# XXXVI

Dear Miss Robins.

Please then let it be THURSDAY at 5. I will take that for granted unless I hear from you otherwise. And I have written to this effect now to Smalley, who had said he would come Wednesday. Thursday I think, will suit him equally and will now suit *me* better. — Here is his note, which I had begun to tear. Please continue the process and throw the morsels into the fire. — You have all my hopes and prayers for to-night. — I am hammering away these mornings at *such* a magnificent play!

Yours ever

Henry James

March 6th [1893]

What with the lively and enlivening testimony borne by budgets of other letters and my own memory of those shining 'Master Builder' days and nights, I find it difficult to readjust the focus to Mr. James's melancholy view of the news we sent after him to Paris — in particular his reading of such news as came from me. I cannot have failed to tell him that the most interesting people in London were coming to see 'The Master Builder' and that many of them were writing entrancing letters about it. How was it possible not to be uplifted when even the little notes scribbled between the Acts would run like this from the forgiving George Moore: 'I thank God I came a second time. It has grown upon me. I understand ... Yours always — ' And again: 'I have come to see the piece for a third time, ... George Moore.'

Would it have been human not to feel one was walking on pink clouds for however little of the long way? As to the next stretch of it, the terrible little drama Mrs. Hugh Bell and I set our hearts on my playing, had found an enthusiastic backer ready to produce it for me in a few weeks' time. It was true that no one in her senses would expect of this particular play that the general public would give it a long run. But I already had experience of the desperation that only breaking away from a long run can appease. There were moreover other negotiations afoot, one dealing with what they used to call a 'society play,' produced later by John Hare.

Charles Hughes was trying to get us to take 'The Master Builder' to Manchester (which ultimately we did), and Mrs. Hugh Bell with my connivance was expressing some of her gaiety and wit in 'The Jerry Builder,' a parody of the play I was appearing in, and Miss Vanbrugh was making ready to do it. Mr. Selwyn Image had been coming to see me about a proposal for a further Ibsen season in London, which would give a glorious chance of doing Rosmersholm and a part of Brand, as well as Hedda and Hilda — and Mrs. Hugh Bell was writing:

'You won't have time to read this at the Theatre, I dare say, but pray read it, then, to-morrow and ruminate on my words of wisdom when I implore you to take care of yourself. I've thought for some days that all these parties and lionizing must be bad for you at this moment. You are

107

doing enough socially to tire you out and your afternoon, Thursday, when you went to H.J. and then worn out to the Theatre, is really enough ...' and I was to come to Yorkshire the moment 'The Master Builder' came to an end.

The worst fault an actress under such conditions had any business to find with life was that there was too much to do and to enjoy. For that reason I was tired, and must have seemed near the end of my physical resources (though, of course, I was not) when Mrs. John Richard Green took me home with her after the last Act one night, and by dint of keeping people away and me in bed till theatre time, enabled the run to be finished before audiences that had every appearance of finding 'The Master Builder' as *forfaerdelig spaendende* as Hilda had.

Among those who, after the last curtain fell, brought their delight and praise behind the scenes, Oscar Wilde's would have been called unmeasured but for the fine air of measure he had the art to lend extravagance. It was true we had not made money, but we were properly grateful for not losing it, and for having gained something no money could bring our way.

## CHAPTER VI

# ALAN'S WIFE
# AND PLAY-GOING WITH
# HENRY JAMES

## XXXVII

*Hotel Westminster,*
*Rue de la Paix,*
*Paris.*
Thursday, [April, '93]

Dear Miss Robins.

I broke away from London at last — but to do it I had to act with such violence and indecorum that it was vain to try to see you once more. Besides, pressed, hunted, fatigued as I knew you to be, it seemed only gentle and generous to stay my hand from your door knocker, and my postage-stamp from your address. I have been haunted with your burdens, and have ached with your aching nerves ever since you told me all you are just now beset by. I don't care to ask you for the last news, because that is asking you for a letter — and yet I am uncomfortable till I know it — know, I mean, how this week will have gone at the Vaudeville — whether there is to be (as I take fully for granted,) another, and whether that horrible spell of non-payment (for you and H.W.) has not at last been broken. If you *can* pencil something on a blue card (only in that case put on 2d. more,) I shall be delighted to get it. Paris is warm and bright —very pretty with spring tints and tones — and it is a pleasure to get from London into a climate. The theatres, however, are not interesting. I hope you are better — with more headway and fewer correspondents. Above all I hope the play holds on. Do let me know, however crudely, the moment anything of any sort happens, and believe me, dear Miss Robins, constantly yours

Henry James

## XXXVIII

*Hotel Westminster,*
*Rue de la Paix,*
*Paris.*
April 7th. [1893]

Dear Miss Robins.

How glad I am to hear from you — but how sorrow-stricken by some of your news! I am divided indeed between compassion for your collapse and gratitude for your wonderful nurses. Please tell them they are my admiration — but not my surprise.

Little indeed do I wonder that your défaillance

came at last — and much more unnatural was it that you should be able to have kept the reckoning back so long. Nothing is so good and so simplifying, sometimes, as a fine complete surrender and I hope with all my heart that you are now rested and reconstructed. I gnash my teeth, however, over the horrid money business — for you and W. — of the play. It is incredible and abominable — I can't think of it or speak of it. Your 'reward' is somewhere (outside of heaven I mean,) and is probably at this moment on its roundabout way to you. May it, however, quickly, quickly arrive. I am sorry, very sorry, that I seem little likely to be present at what you are doing for the 'Independent' — if it takes [place?] soon, as I suppose. I am in the dark as yet about the length of my stay abroad — it depends upon the movements of other people. But there is a strong appearance that I shall be back in town by the middle of May; though this was not at all my original programme. Paris is wonderful just now — for weather, climate, beauty &c. — a strange (and alarming) anticipated June. But it is otherwise exceptionally uninteresting — the theatre, in particular, in almost complete eclipse — failures, miseries, stupidities — very much like London and without an Ibsen or a Robins. I saw a few nights ago a representation at the Français which was of a mediocrity I had never before seen achieved there. As you know, I take it, by this time, they are all going over to Drury Lane for June; and I bespeak hereby your company (if you will confer it, and *if I am then in town!!* — an important proviso) for as many of the performances as you will allow me to conduct you to. Is it understood? I shall most probably be in town. And this without illusions as to their prospects in London in these particular and actual conditions — conditions which, I predict, will engender disaster and failure. Several years ago, when they had a lot of brilliant people they have now lost, they *just* got on at the Gaiety. Shorn now, distinctly, of several of their attractions and of *some* of their prestige, they won't fill the vast Drury Lane — or anything approaching it.

Hence recriminations, humiliations, acrimonies, catastrophes — you will see it all. The British public doesn't care a *straw* for French acting — it only cares for Sarah B. But the others will play, at any rate, to you and me. I am having a very quiet busy time and am pegging away hard at the drama. I shall have acts and things to read you — if you will listen to them. Do let me have an echo, meanwhile, — if you have time — of anything that may be going in London. I should like to ask for some details about your present job — but I dread to impose burdens on your weariness. Are the Achurches tending upward — or still further downward? But I believe last night determined that and I shall consult the feuilles publiques. One thing I do wish you would do — tell me 3 words about Oscar W's piece — when it is produced; and if in particular the *sub-*

*ject* seems to discount my poor 3-year-older (or almost,) that Hare will neither produce nor part with. If you are still with Mrs Bell — and I gather you will be — please express to her all my sentiments. Your account of Mrs Green's ministrations brings tears to my eyes. Brava, as we say here, Mrs Green. Brava everyone! Please don't be any more silent than sounds *well*, and believe me, dear Miss Robins yours always

Henry James

When the private initiators of a series of Ibsen Subscription performances had their first meeting, I was in Yorkshire. But I was present some days later at the little House of Commons dinner when the Edward Greys and their guests — among them Mr. Asquith, then Home Secretary, later Premier and Lord Oxford and Asquith; Mr. [later Lord] Haldane; Mrs. John Richard Green [later member of the Irish Senate] and Mr. Alfred [later Lord] Milner — promised to become subscribers and were as good as their word.

The *Westminster Gazette* ended a reference to the project:

'Mrs. J. R. Green and Sir Frederick Pollock, Bart., have been appointed to act as trustees of the funds, and cheques should be sent to Mrs. Green, 14 Kensington Square ... Among the names of guarantors already enrolled, in addition to those mentioned above, were Lady Pollock, Lady Lyttelton, Lady Manners, Miss Margot Tennant, Mr. Fuller Maitland, Mrs. Hugh Bell, Mr. Oscar

Wilde, Mr. Crackanthorpe Q.C., and Mr. Oswald Crawfurd.'

## XXXIX

Dear Mrs Bell.

Just 3 words — to thank you for your news — and to 'reassure' you, as you kindly express it, by saying that my absence from England is indeed to be *not* long, inasmuch as owing to a fundamental change (for 'family' reasons!) in my projects, I have reason to believe that I shall be back in London, provisionally at all events, by the mid-May, at latest. Is, by the same token, Miss Elizabeth to be, 'mid-May's eldest child'? I mean is she to begin to re-Ibsenize about that moment? I should like to know — very much — all about the probable date and other conditions — and whether the five hundred guineas are really to be looked for to flow in, &c. Any crumb of information on these thrilling themes that you could flick towards me with an idle finger would be trappée au passage! And any stray crust or two about Oscar's play and the next declaration (by the same Miss E.) of Independence would be equally gobbled. Do tell me about the Independent thing — I haven't a ray of light on it. And *don't* neglect Oscar! Neglect your children, rather, *for* him! What I regretted

114

was not so much the fact of the mere ('mere', as it were!) re-Ibsenizing, as of the 'mere' necessity for that — and that only. Oh yes — when that loathsome —— is preferred! La vie est trop laide as we say here. And yet we haven't a ——! And we *have* the loveliest Paris I have almost ever seen. As Paris is France, you too must also be happy. Mille compliments empressés, chère Madame.　　Henry James

In replying to Mr. Henry James's request for news, Mrs. Hugh Bell enclosed a copy of the prospectus, and suggested that he should allow his name to be added to the list.

The circular was as follows:—

A desire having been expressed in many quarters that this season should not pass without a revival of 'Hedda Gabler' and some further representations of 'The Master Builder,' a committee has been formed for the purpose of organizing a series of Subscription Performances (both Matinées and Evening Performances) to be given during the month of June, of these plays, of 'Rosmersholm,' and, if possible, of one of Ibsen's poetic dramas in each of which Miss Elizabeth Robins and Mr. Herbert Waring will appear.

The estimated expense of ten or twelve performances being about 500 guineas, it is proposed to raise this sum in 100 subscriptions of five guineas each, without further liability. This will entitle each subscriber to seats to the value of five guineas at the current Theatrical Rates, and in the event of a profit being realized in the per-

formances, a return will be made to the subscribers.

A meeting of those interested in this undertaking was held on the 13th inst., at the house of
Mrs. J. R. Green, 14 Kensington Square, W., for
the purpose of taking the preliminary steps of
organization.

Mrs. J. R. Green and Sir Frederick Pollock,
Bart., have kindly consented to act as trustees of
the funds, and cheques may be sent to Mrs. Green,
as soon as possible, in order to allow time for the
necessary preparations and rehearsals.

Further particulars will be announced in due
course.

## XL

*Hotel Westminster,*
*Rue de la Paix,*
Friday [April 18th, 1893]

Dear Mrs Bell.

I enclose a cheque for £5. 5. 0 as I suppose that
is the essential. I suppose further that I am as
delighted with the undertaking of ces dames as I
can be with anything that so much *commits* Miss
Robins to figure to the public as an Ibsen-actress
only. However it is doubtless as well to be that as
any of the other 'only's' that seem open to others
of the profession. It seems always, at best, a case of
an 'only'. Therefore let me rejoice in the I trust
rapidly organizing series. Please express to her all
my exultation and sympathy. The great thing is
that it shouldn't take so much of her health to start

116

them as it took to start the 'Master-Builder.' Do keep her from getting rid of it at any more than her *usual* rate. This beggarly £5. 5. 0. seems very little — but I shall pay for as many seats *more* at the time — as I can manage — and shall economise on the Comédie Française — which is decidedly malade. I am so delighted she (the Comédie Scandinave) is still with you. Many greetings. Great is the haste of yours, dear Mrs Bell, most truly,

Henry James

'Oscar W.'s tragedy' was 'A Woman of No Importance,' produced at the Haymarket on April 19th.

Mr. James's request for 'a crumb of betrayal' of the 'Independent Conspiracy' refers to one of the enterprises of that true lover of the stage and generous patron, Mr. J. T. Grein, founder and manager of the Independent Theatre. The English public already owed to him, among other debts, the first hearing given to Ibsen's 'Ghosts.' He had recently welcomed my suggestion that, in the interval before our Ibsen Series was due at another theatre, he should produce an anonymous play, 'Alan's Wife,' with a company of my choosing. This is the play referred to, all-unsuspectingly, by Mr. James as the 'dramatic gem.'

Mr. St. John Ervine has lately said of this 'gem' that it 'caused a terrific rumpus ... Terms as fierce as those that had been applied to Ibsen's "Ghosts" after its first appearance in London, were applied to the piece.'

Certainly it furnished ground for a spirited

encounter among the Three Musketeers of the Drama of that day — Walkley, Archer and Shaw. Controversy raged round the question of authorship of the play, and ink continued to be spilt on the dreadfulness of the theme. Apart from printed accounts in the book of the play (published by Mr. J. T. Grein) and later references in the *Saturday Review* by Mr. Shaw, two or three records survive of the longer duel between those two staunch friends, Shaw and Archer, who hurled insulting letters at each other — and neither a penny the worse. The little piece saw the light on April 28th, 1893. Under date November 10th, 1928, on the flyleaf of a copy of the book Mr. Shaw, after a rest of thirty-five years, had another 'go' at poor 'Alan's Wife.' For sake of this letter which I have never seen, the book was 'collected' by Mr. Gabriel Wells, who found himself echoing to the ears of Mr. St. John Ervine (then in New York) the old inquiry: 'Who wrote "Alan's Wife"?' Mr. Ervine in his turn passed the question on to the writer of the fly-leaf letter. So it was that some thirty-six years after 'Alan's Wife' was produced, Mr. Bernard Shaw was sending a cable message across the Atlantic: 'Do not know author but suspect Miss Robins she knows Bernard Shaw.'

Lady Bell, in my presence, privately confided the well-kept secret to Mr. Grein, on a certain public occasion. It was during the banquet given a few years ago in honour of the founder of the Independent Theatre. Among the hundreds gathered were some with faithful memories who knew that Mr. Grein's services had never been, probably never could be, fully appraised. It was a critical hour in dramatic history when Mr. Grein produced Ibsen's most revolutionary play. 'Ghosts' was then and for long after not only bitterly denounced but loathed and *feared*. It was, of course, rejected with horror by the Censor. No one knew better than Mr. Grein that 'Ghosts' could not make money. No one knew so well that its producer risked his official and business position and his post as dramatic critic. If he never risked as much afterward it was only because he never again held in his hands so shining an apple of discord. He continued unrepentant through the years, offering hospitality to plays that he thought well of, plays that but for him had little or no chance of seeing the light.

To say that Bernard Shaw's fate hung on Mr. Grein sounds far stranger to-day than it would in '92. The reason is that few but Mr. Grein, and absolutely no manager, could think of Shaw then as a dramatist of the future. To his honour, he was no philanderer with playwriting. He meant business, and the realist in G.B.S. would have lacked any valid encouragement to waste his time on a new, precarious profession if, at the right moment, he had not been given his first hearing.

Naturally there were other, less fine, feathers than the Shaw plume in Mr. Grein's cap at the banquet some thirty years later. One little feather, quite invisible to most, was none the less presuming to wave, a fact that two of the guests pointed out to each other while the throng streamed toward the door.

In that generous air, full of waving and nodding and acknowledgments, Lady Bell stood a moment, offering Mr. Grein thanks long overdue, for his enterprise, his gallant enthusiasm, in giving a hearing to a nameless work. He had called it in print: 'One of the truest tragedies ever written by an Englishman.'

'We wrote "Alan's Wife," ' said Lady Bell.

## XLI

*Hotel Westminster,*
*Rue de la Paix,*
*Paris.*
April 21st. [1893]

Dear Miss Robins.

It is only the overwhelming stress of Paris that has kept me from writing to you any one of these last days. Words of cordial sympathy have been on my pen's end ever since Mrs. Bell sent me the prospectus of the new Ibsen series. I rejoice with you over this as vociferously as I *can* rejoice over an episode which, with a 100 merits, has the defect of committing you to the public eye more and more as an Ibsen-actress only! Of course I know it's only for an hour — therefore the flaw in the perfection doesn't make me very unhappy, and I am writing now only to assure you of my very earnest and fundamental participation of spirit. If I ask you if the scheme is taking maturer form I simply give you, of course, a chance to say 'Come and see!' You are of course too busy to make it fair to 'ask' you anything whatsoever — even for a crumb of betrayal of your

'Independent' conspiracy or a spark of ecstasy over Oscar W's tragedy. I am consumed with curiosity about each — but I eat my heart out in silence. I *am* coming to see, at the 1st possible moment. In the meanwhile my greatest interest, after all, is, I think, in your health — with a good deal added for your frock — in the forthcoming picture.* Do let them both be a perfect fit! I wrote to you at Redcar — a good while ago. Yours, dear Miss Robins, always

Henry James

* * * *

In the following letter: 1. 'Dorset St' stands for Manchester Square Mansions, otherwise 'Morocco,' or by its newer and more lasting name borrowed from the 'Master Builder,' 'The Luftslot' — castle in the air. The context runs:

HILDA

We two will set to work together. And then we will build the loveliest — the very loveliest — thing in all the world.

SOLNESS

(*Intently*) Hilda — tell me what that is . . . the loveliest thing in the world that we two are to build together?

HILDA

(*Silent a little while, then with an indefinable expression in her eyes*). Castles in the air.

* This was not an Ibsen lady, but Alan's wife.

SOLNESS

(*Rises*) After this day we two will build together, Hilda.

HILDA

(*With a half dubious smile*) A *real* castle in the
air?

SOLNESS

Yes. One with a firm foundation under it . . .
for now I see it. Men have no use for these homes
of theirs to be happy in . . . And I shouldn't have
had any use for such a home, if I had had one. . . .

HILDA

Then you will never build anything more?

SOLNESS

(*With animation*) On the contrary, I am just
going to begin.

HILDA

What then? What will you build? Tell me,
quickly.

SOLNESS

I believe there is only one possible dwelling-
place for human happiness. . . .

HILDA

(*Jubilant, clapping her hands*) Oh, Mr. Solness . . .! My lovely, lovely castle. Our castle in the
air.

\*  \*  \*  \*

2. 'Tomorrow night' was to see the production
of 'Alan's Wife.'

122

## XLII

*Hotel Westminster,*
this Thursday. [27th April, 1893]

Dear Mrs Bell.

I owe you better thanks for your charming and interesting letter than I can manage to seize the occasion to convey to you adequately. The very Paris we commemorate, and adore, and regret, smothers me with its superincumbent presence. Yes, it's the same old splendid, amiable monster — but from having had more of it, the last 16 years than you, I suppose, I am less à l'abri from satiety with it. I am suffering at present from that luxurious complaint, and as I shall have been here next Wednesday 7 weeks I go on Tuesday to Lucerne (!!) after which (I suppose!) I return to England. I figure you to-day climbing the Jacob's ladder of Dorset St. (1), as a kind of an angel of a country cousin. To-morrow night (2) will see me, like the summer evening — the 'holy time' — in Wordsworth 'as quiet as a nun' — for fear of breaking the spell you will, I devoutly hope, je vous en *conjure* be sitting under. If it *is* broken, send me at least the pieces. If it isn't send me the whole thing. Excuse the presumptuous familiarity of these commands, je vous en supplie, madame. I hope the declaration of Independence may help the declaration of Dependence — the appeal for subscriptions for the series. — If you have a hearing of the entrancing

123

Oscar may I have an echo of it? I read with wonderment Archer's strange rhapsody over him in the *World*. However, I sit in darkness. Perhaps you'll tell me who the Friday play is *by?* Au revoir, chère Madame. Excuse the reluctant brevity of yours always

Henry James

## XLIII

*Hotel Westminster,*
*Rue de la Paix*
*Paris.*

Sunday. [April 30th 1893].

Dear Miss Robins.

Those ladies have written me the delightful news of your magnificent success — and their emotion is so contagious that I overflow into this immediate assurance — to yourself — that nothing at this moment could have given me greater pleasure. They both put it superlatively and Mrs. Clifford is admirably copious. She consoles me a little — by her vividness — for my detestable absence from the scene. The battle is won and the country is evidently yours. I am particularly happy you are going to do it again. Yet what a misery is 'again' — when again is only once or twice! You *must* do it, somehow or other, after I get back. May it be a wondrous thing for the Ibsen plan — obviously it can't help being. I go on Wednesday to Switzerland — for a short time — and thence come back to De Vere Gardens. I hope greatly not to miss the Duse — to get there for her 2nd week. You must go with me — often. Please again believe in my most superlative satisfaction.

Yours, dear Miss Robins, always

Henry James

## XLIV

*H. Westminster,*
Sunday
[30th April, 1893]

Dear Mrs Bell.

I am profusely obliged to you, and I rejoice greatly. It must have been very fine and very strange and very satisfactory and very encouraging and promoting. I have written to congratulate her — and I hope with all my heart there will prove to have been some such measurable *effect* to congratulate her *on,* that one's words won't simply sit smiling in the void — like effusive guests longing for the announcement of dinner. *Do* let me know if ANY fume of the possible repast finds its way to your supersensitive nostril. Meanwhile there is something in the reckless 'fun', as it were, of being simply glad of her having scored. I gather from your letter and from a word from Mrs Clifford — in fact a dithyramb — that she scored very heavily. The play sounds primitive — but the primitive is sometimes the sublime. Why so much mystery about it? But *nurse* the mystery if it

125

helps. *I* haven't a glimmer of knowledge. I didn't mean to ask you — tiraillée and tremballée as you must be, a sole question. It was most good of you to find a moment to scribble me. I hope the thing will be repeated more than once and the other thing *wafted* by it. I leave Paris on Wednesday — but not yet for London. Yours most gratefully

Henry James

The reference towards the end of the previous letter and the subject of this one, is Mr. George Alexander's offer of the part of 'The Second Mrs. Tanqueray.'

## XLV

*H. Westminster,*
Monday
[May 1st 1893]

Dear Mrs Bell.

Que me dites-vous là? How exceedingly delightful and how very kindly inspired you have been to let me have it in the bright intensity of a 'wire'! I shall probably flash gratefully back at you as soon as I can go round the corner! but please let this meanwhile (the 'meanwhile' is of course only to tromper *my* impatience,) express to you my happy agitation. Oh, one must be back for *that!* I wrote to you yesterday. I hope tremendously she gets good terms. But vogue la galère.

Yours more theatrically than ever — ce que c'est de nous!

Henry James

P.S. My address will be after to-morrow:
  *Hotel National, Lucerne.*

The part of Mrs. Tanqueray was, or would have been, offered originally to Mrs. Patrick Campbell. She, at the moment, was still engaged at the Adelphi. When that bar was removed the part reverted to her. Mr. James was too far away to understand the simplicity of the situation, or to foresee in the issue, its justification. None the less, or perhaps all the more, his partisanship was balm.

XLVI

*Paris:*<br>Wednesday.<br>[May 2nd, 1893]

Dear Mrs Bell.

Your letter just catches me here. Strange and passing sad is your story. What an abominable — what an atrocious, imbroglio — and how admirably well she behaved! Please assure her of the intensity of my sentiments over it. But what endless perversities and treacheries of fate! And a pupil of G. R. Sim's *instead* of her! This world is really pour rire and the most vitriolic irony is as mother's milk to the satire one would *like* to lash it with. But, all the

127

same, the episode is full to overflowing of point; and what you say about it true to the letter. Thank you for such kind and explicit renseignements. There are new possibilities in the air — and from one day to the other they will break out. The train is smouldering for a conflagration — and *any* spark may light it. I gather she is scattering sparks by the thousand. I don't console myself for not seeing the new part. But I rejoice still more greatly in the sustained and renewed impression. Will you very kindly express these things to her for yours — and hers, dear Mrs Bell, most truly

Henry James

The Ibsen series had hardly ended before the French series of that year began. Mr. James and I were among those who assisted at the first performance of 'Un Père Prodigue' by the company of the Comédie Française.

The note that follows, dealing, like so many, with similar arrangements, is undated. One such will do as well as another to 'place' what had come to be Mr. James's practice of associating me with his theatre-going.

No. XLVII belongs, I rather think, to the French season of the previous year, when we saw Bernhardt once at least and Coquelin five times.

It is forgivable, I hope, to admit that going with Mr. James to English plays sometimes demanded what our Florida cook would call 'de bol' courage.'

One never grew wholly acclimatized to the nipping airs that now and then would blow about

the startled stalls. Mr. James's all too audible remarks, conveyed in terms always 'chosen' often
singularly picturesque, sometimes diabolic, as
though he revelled in mercilessness — would send
cold shivers down his companion's spine. She
could tell without looking, that the lucky people
on each side, or immediately in front or behind —
whether they, 'poor dears,' were enjoying the play
or not — very certainly were enjoying Mr. James.
As for me, at such times I could only sit tingling
under a series of shocks. To remonstrate however
discreetly made things worse. From a denuncia-
tion so 'lively' that it was deadly, the critic would
fall to a still more scathing pity, in which I would
find myself involved.

It was a different matter when the play was
French or Italian, and not always, I used to think,
because it was actually so much better. The alien
tongue, the nature as well as the Art of the Latin,
appealed strongly to Henry James; they found
his guard down. He could 'give' himself to the
foreign actor as I never saw him so much as begin
to do in the case of anyone speaking English.

I remember a moment between the Acts of
'Chamillac' when in his eager explanation and
enforcement I realized with a jolt of incredulity
that never once in the entire repertory had the
smallest hole been picked in Coquelin. Mr. James
was actually content merely to 'follow' and
enjoy!!

Yet not entirely content until he had done all
in his power to carry his guest along with him.
It was as though he couldn't, in courtesy, leave
her so far behind if it could be helped. In that
way it came about, out of his desire to enable me

to distinguish, that I learned how little of Coquelin's art, of his temperamental responsiveness, his wit, his subtlety, his triumphant technique were wasted on Henry James.

He would not of course expect that I should rise to his heights of analytic appreciation — yet he may have thought more was lost on me than was always the case. The sheer *pace* in much of French stage utterance would sometimes leave me far behind, as is shown in a note of mine to Mrs. Hugh Bell, which if allowed to stand as witness, must be left in all its original crudity. The lines are written in pencil and dated only, 'Friday midnight, or after.

'My dear my dear, I've had a wonderful evening! Huge sensations and a beautiful time. I think I said nothing, however, and it occurs to me that Mr. James doesn't realize how enchanted I was. However, I was too busy drinking it in at the time and *feeling* it afterwards, to think about him. It was superb — superb. And yet in Coquelin's strongest and most daring bit [!] of passion I didn't like him — it was where he breaks out at the thought of substituting for Fabienne some one who has a child, I think — at least it comes before his speech about the woman of the town — "She is a human being." This last I thought *tremendous* — the other, intended apparently to be even more impulsive, struck me as false and "tricky." But, oh, it was all so interesting, so brilliant, so inspiring! . . .' Another pencil scrawl:

'H.J. was in one of his most agreeable moods. I enjoyed the evening in spite of the play . . . my kind compatriot is going to take me to see Duse next week. I live on the thought of it. Oh, I'm glad that woman is in the world —'

and then a refusal to be definite in the matter of dinner-party dates, because:

'I haven't seen Duse's further plans announced — or I'd know better what night Mr. James would be likely to propose. He means, I think, to see "La Femme de Claude." Oh, why am I not going every blessed night? . . .'

a question that seems to have been answered by having my heart's desire.

Mr. James's first gift to me — his novel of the stage, 'The Tragic Muse' — might better have prepared an actress for some of his judgments. His praise — using the word not so much in the ordinary sense as meaning appraisement — of French acting did in one instance astonish and bewilder me. In his talks about the Théâtre Français I used to hear about Delaunay, Got, Régnier, Croizette, Mounet Sully and the rest.

The greater people were unfortunately dead. Sarah and Coquelin had seceded. But still the Français maintained a level unapproachable elsewhere. He improvised a 'Who's Who' among the outstanding French actors of the day. I asked about the women. Bartet was catalogued and a certain Mlle Reichemberg, as I remember for two reasons, neither very intelligent. One, because her name was so extremely un-French, in spite of Mr. James's delicate gallicizing; and the other reason was that she kept her position as the darling of the Comédie because she kept her figure. This lady went on playing ingénues decade after decade because there wasn't in all France an actress as young as Mlle Reichemberg in her sixties. It was a pity I myself had arrived too late on the scene to see her, but there was Bartet: 'I would like you to observe Bartet.' In his grave, spare account, long before she reached London, I 'observed' Bartet with might and main. So much was clear: the actress approved by Mr. James without parentheses, or qualification, must indeed be tremendous so far as tremendousness was compatible with a highly fastidious dramatic intelligence trained in that supreme school.

It was during the week following the Ibsen Series that I was taken to see Bartet — an occasion tense with excitement. For the leading actress of the first Theatre in the world was to make her appearance in that play I had so waited for, worked for, battled for and lost.

One of the strange experiences in retracing steps where the foot has left no print, is my seeing Bartet play 'Denise.' That I actually did see her is a fact set down plainly in an Engagement Book. But in my unworthy memory not a wrack remains. Nowhere so much as an echo of my disappointment. I seem to have taken it that I had *not* seen 'Denise' though I had seen a very graceful, discreet presence who was Mme Bartet. I cannot imagine what was possible to say to Mr. James and there I leave it — as perhaps I, all helplessly, left it that June night in '93.

The strange thing is that I cannot so easily leave the other 'Denise' — the one I never saw. I seem still to remember the first night Duse played the part in Rome, though I have not been in Rome. I am moved afresh at thought of all the fine devotion Duse lavished, all that passion of feeling, that power to make you share in the delight and the anguish of living — gone as utterly

as the noise of shouting in the Roman street —
'Duse!' 'Duse!' — and yet it is that I hear in the
silence Mme Bartet left behind.

## XLVII

34 *De Vere Gardens, W.*
Tuesday. [1893]

Dear Miss Robins.

What more natural than that, having had an ice
and a wafer with you, I should duplicate the order,
as they say in the U.S., with your double? I probably thought it was still *you* — and the same old ice
— and even the same old wafer. Please take care
that it be you, however, and not Mrs ——, that I go
to the play with on the 1st. Between Serpent Sarah
and Serpent Muriel (isn't that her name?) I should
think of Eve, in Eden, as not '*in* it!' — I rejoice that
you approve Saturday week; and hope very much
you will come and dine with me — very slightly, 1st.
I will give you a further reminder.

Yours always
Henry James

In the Strand would be, at least, plenty of
shouting.

To the Adelphi — after that incongruous preface of Coquelin and the dim discreet Bartet — I
was returning, for Henry Pettitt's new melodrama
and a few weeks' fat salary, before beginning a
year's engagement under John Hare at the Garrick.

## XLVIII

*2, Wellington Crescent, Ramsgate,*
Monday, July 4 '93.

Dear Mrs Bell.

Most kind and most punctual your tribute to my curiosity *in re* Adelphi idiocy. Your report is very much what I expected, and the result only freshly proves and confirms the old so intensely solid moral that out of a sow's ear no silk purse can be made by *anyone*. In a bad play *every*thing is bad; just as there is no such thing as a 'good part' in such a play, so there is in a bad part no such thing as *any* stuff to conjure with. The only thing is to do what one can for it and leave the responsibility with the author. But I hope Miss R. doesn't 'feel badly' about having set her foot dans cette galère. I hope this especially because I so frankly gave my voice for her doing so when she asked me. My view of *why* was, to my sense, the right one; it seems to me the right one still, — absolutely — just as much, and if I had to advise her again I should do so in just the same way. It would be worth her having done it if only to have elicited such a 'document' as the grotesquely-malignant observations I just see in the *Daily Telegraph*. What a slimy little worm is the author of those remarks; yet contributing to the gaiety of nations by his delicious account of the way the trembling Ibsenites forced Mrs Lonsdale and Miss Robins upon the awful Pettitt, lest, without those

compromising associates the said Pettitt should too
uttterly annihilate Ibsen! Basta! — though the world
has *du bon,* after all. What do you want of your
talent for parody? The parodies are so ready-made
and stare one in the face. Still, I should like one of
your 4 hours at Datchet — is that the muse's shrine?
Will you show this — if you have a convenient
chance — to Miss Robins — to testify to my interest?
I don't want to harceler her, tired as she is, with
letters.

Oh, the peace of Ramsgate! pas la moindre muse!

Yours most truly

Henry James

## XLIX

*34 De Vere Gardens, W.*
Thursday.
[July or Aug. 1893]

Dear Miss Robins.

I am in London again after a vast absence, and
nothing that it contains presents itself to me more
imperatively than the opportunity of seeing you
again. I shall do so from a stall of vantage only, I am
afraid, next week — Monday or Tuesday; but my
impatience will be easier to live with if I am able to
arrive at a 'private interview' sooner. The talk of
the town is that you are living at Wimbledon. Is it
so — and is it a thing one may presume on? Should
you be at home there on Sunday afternoon — and

135

may I come out and see you? I probably dine there — i.e. at Wimbledon — at 7:30 or 8 in that day —and might I come for a cup of tea to *your* bower? *Is* Mrs Green the fair Rosamund whom you have constructed it for? At any rate I only want the clue to arrive.

Yours and Mrs Green's most truly

Henry James

## CHAPTER VII

# À LA GUERRE COMME À LA GUERRE

On November 27th comes the first reference in writing to those two plays we had talked about so often, 'Guy Domville,' and the light comedy 'for Daly' — that is to say for Ada Rehan.

L

*34 De Vere Gardens, W.*
Monday.
[Nov. 27, 1893]

Dear Miss Robins.

I shall look out for you feverishly to-morrow at the Abbey Chapterhouse. I am so glad — for dear Lowell's honoured memory — that you are going.

It is sad that we are so whirled along — but I hope there will be occasions — when the Garrick holiday comes. I shan't have any very novel 'play-news' for you, I fear — though I have to-day been in conference with St. James's scene-painters (and Alfred

Parsons, their inspirer;) and work at Daly's on my other play begins to-morrow. I want on my side to be shown *your* horizons.

I hope you are robust.

Yours always<br>Henry James

## LI

34 De Vere Gardens, W.<br>Thursday.<br>[Nov. 30, 1893]

Dear Miss Robins.

The ——s are very worthy people — he with the worth of County Cork, she with that of the State of —— who will do you no harm at all save perhaps that of pursuing and inviting you too much. I don't *revel* in them — but there are drearier folk. I prefer, for instance (in strict confidence), an hour of —— to a cycle of ——! On the other hand I don't remember *when* I so far succumbed — or grew demoralized — as to arrange with him, for a descent — or an ascent — upon you! It is true there are moments when one arranges *anything* to be quiet — and get away!

I looked for you — vainly — at the Abbey till my eyes protruded from my head — and yet you passed near me! It was too discreet a passage. I wish indeed I were free on Wednesday p.m.— I mean in the evening. But I perversely dine out. I am very sorry — I should like so much to converse with you — am indeed particularly desirous to do so. Should you be free at 5 — 5.30 — (the former preferred) that (Wednesday) afternoon — or any other afternoon next week (save Thursday) I would come with great pleasure if you can mention one.

No, alas, I am not in rehearsal yet — though they have begun, or are just beginning I believe, some intensely private preliminaries at Daly's — which make me very uneasy. At the St. James's I am only at the point of Scenery and clothes — Alfred Parsons or Percy Anderson — all very lovely indeed. I will describe them to you!

Yours always<br>Henry James

## LII

The Athenæum,<br>Wednesday 2 p.m.<br>[Dec. 6th 1893]

Dear Miss Robins.

Only a word to say that the result (for your very sympathetic ear,) of the ghastly — yes, it's the word! — two hours I have just brought to a close at Daly's is that I write to him to-night to withdraw my piece. The 'rehearsal' left me in such a state of nervous exasperation that I judged it best — or rather I could only control myself and trust myself enough — to say simply to him after the last word was spoken: 'I shall take some hours to become perfectly clear to myself as to the reflections which this occasion — taken in connection with your note of Saturday, causes me to make. And then I will write to you — and then to walk out of the theatre. To Ada Rehan (white, haggard, ill-looking almost in *anguish*) I couldn't bring myself to *speak*. I know Bourchier and said goodbye to him — but I was not given a single *second's* opportunity of having the least contact or word with any other member of the company; who began and stammeringly *read* their parts the instant I came in, and vanished the instant the 3rd Act ended. Don't pity me too much — rather rejoice with

Yours always<br>Henry James

## LIII

[On envelope]
Don't answer, positively.

*34 De Vere Gardens, W.*
Dec. 6th [1893]

Dear Mrs Bell.

Miss Robins tells me you have gone and this is a wail of despair. Please believe in my great discomfiture at not having seen you before your flight. From day to day I desired and designed it — but I was lapped in a false security. I thought that last talk of ours was a pledge that you were to stay and stay: at any rate till the 20th or thereabouts. I think you

FROM A PHOTOGRAPH OF LADY BELL, THE LAST TAKEN
BEFORE HER DEATH IN 1931

mentioned a date — but I forgot it. So I live only with my eyes on your return. May Providence — or Hugo * — speed it: to say nothing of Miss Elizabeth. The latter has been a comfort to me ces-jours-ci on the occasion of a horrid désagrément — my withdrawing from Daly (provoked thereto by his calculated — or calculating — arts,) the play he has had from this last twelve month, and was (in my candid vision,) to have produced a month hence. He is an abyss — but not an abyss of interest. Therefore basta. But Miss Elizabeth will give you a few thrilling details over the Redcar plumpuddings. The life on the glorious planches seems even more fraught with Danger than a life on the ocean wave! But I am, after all, safe and sound. I wish I could think the same of you.† I have again and again thought with every sympathy of your so bravely borne infirmity since you so touchingly told me. May Xmas tromper it a little and my penmanship not rub it too much the wrong way.

Always yours<br>Henry James

* Hugo was Lady Bell's only son.
† Mrs. Hugh Bell's eyesight was seriously threatened.

# LIV

Dear Miss Robins.

All thanks for your sympathy — but don't *think* of the matter more. The thing is over, and well over (in the sense of *utterness,*) and I take nothing but comfort in the result. It shakes, miserably, I confess, the *general* comfort (small and minutely shakable as that has hitherto been,) of my connection — potential — with the stage. But fortunately I am incurable in that perverse tendency and I shall live, probably, to be as much disconcerted and deluded yet again. But for the present, before twelve days are spent, I shall be more than ready to be consoled by the liveliness of our little private theatricals on the 18th.

No word yet from Carr — but it is much too soon. I shan't begin and look till next Monday. I am writing a word to Mrs Bell to tell her how I deplore that she departed before I saw her again.— I have begun another play! But I think I told you.

Yours always

Henry James

## LV

*34 De Vere Gardens, W.*
Thursday.
[14th Dec., 1893]

Dear Mrs Bell.

It was very gentle and graceful of you to squander your hoarded moyens on answering my note; and as one good turn deserves a bad one, behold I send you more matter for perusal, *but absolutely not for response.* Nothing would induce me to inflict upon you the recital of the Daly provocations — but you shall have them for the Redcar Xmas week — in the spacious times of great Elizabeth. *She* will retail to you what she has patiently listened to — matter for a roaring Xmas fire. Ouf! — it's a relief to be able to stop so painfully pretending (for good manners) that one takes the poor blundered and muddled Daly enterprise seriously. In our trade are there *enough* ways of suffering, hein?

Ah, you must not wait to come in only with March — though you will have every right to come in like a lion. You went out much too much — the other day — like a lamb! Brave and beautiful, learned and lovely Hugo — please give him my love. Pile the Yule logs high and the salt into the brandy — to make snapdragon. Buon' divertimento!

Yours and everyone's, evermore
Henry James

The last I saw of Mr. James that year ('93) was just before I went away for the holidays. He came, as the Engagement Book says, 'with play' on the 18th of December.

On my return to London, in January, a mention of play-going with him occurs in a letter to Mrs. Hugh Bell. To explain what I reported, the fact should be recalled that an unusual number of women at that period were writing plays.

Mrs. Hugh Bell apart — for 'apart' is what she was, in her particular field, as Mr. James was quick to acknowledge — among his friends and mine tempting fortune at Stage doors, were Mrs. Montague Crackanthorpe, Miss Constance Fletcher ('George Fleming' author of 'Kismet,' etc.), Mrs. E. S. Willard, Mme. Vandervelde, wife of the Belgian Minister, and others, besides those who had won a hearing: Mrs. W. K. Clifford; Mrs. Craigie ('John Oliver Hobbs'), 'Michael Field,' 'Elin Ameen,' Miss Florence Warden, Mrs. de la Pasture, Lady Colin Campbell, Lady Violet Greville and again, 'others.'

In spite of all this activity — because of it, Mr. James might and probably did say — and despite the scant harvest after so much sowing, there was a widespread conviction, which for all I know may still persist, that no woman can write a good full-length play.

For some months I had been urging the claims of Miss Constance Fletcher, and had introduced a play of hers to more than one manager. Mr. John Hare, in whose theatre Mr. James and I were sitting, had Miss Fletcher's play under consideration at that moment.

'While we were being bored by Grundy's play,'

144

my report ran, to F. B., Jan. 15, 'I turned to Henry James and said: "When I write *my* great play there are three words I won't have in it." "*Your* great play?" he said with a start, and a look of horror . . . Then a little reassured by my expression, he asked: "What words?" "Twenty years ago," I said, and he agreed solemnly that they should be cut out of *any*body's "great play." Also that fat ladies in caps should NEVER have a past . . .' and tranquillity was restored.

As little as my companion, could I conceive my making a claim on his patience for a play of my own, still less his receiving it with the lively and helpful interest to which a later letter bears witness.

1894, in addition to his visits abroad, was admittedly for Mr. James a very full year. The only clue in the published letters to the kind of work he was chiefly doing is given in a couple of sentences written on December 29th, 1893, in which he sums up the recent experience with his Daly play: But à la guerre comme à la guerre. I mean to wage this war ferociously for one year more — 1894 —'

In letter LVI, my coming 'back to work' is a reference to the play by Constance Fletcher, already referred to. 'Mrs. Lessingham,' was produced at the Garrick on April 7th, and played in by John Hare, Forbes Robertson, Kate Rorke, Gerald du Maurier, myself and others.

From Venice Mr. James found time to write about the favourable reception.

145

## LVI

*34 De Vere Gardens, W.*
March 7th, [1894]

Dear Miss Robins.

I should sooner have thanked you for your note had I not been these three days very miserable with a little malady that has made it a sadness to sit up and write. I am better to-day and nursing the remainder of my melancholy so as to qualify it for keeping this p.m. an engagement to dine. I'm afraid you won't be there — more's the pity. But I have been notified of where you will be on Saturday afternoon, and hope to squeeze a sympathetic presence into the jubilant mass. If I don't succeed please know it is because I shall not have been well enough. But I shall insist on being. I rejoice that you come back to work, and I hope with all my heart that the work will be very fruitful. I go abroad (I hope and fear) the end of next week and I must arrange with you for a talk before that (if we don't manage it on Saturday.)

I'm sorry to hear of Mrs Bell 'far from well' — and shall try to see her. I shall be more easily silent about her new work as I shouldn't in the least know what to say about it.

May the smell of your paint grow less! It makes me feel fearfully dirty to hear of your purifications. I can't afford to be clean. My only hope of it is if Miss Fletcher will write me a play. I hope Hare is better and benevolent — though that is really very generous of me. Vale.

Yours, dear Miss Robins, always

Henry James

P.S.   My photog. was taken in the act of seeing you rehearse: don't you see that in it?

## LVII

*Casa Biondetti,*
*San Vio, 715,*
*Venice.*

April 12th. [1894]

Dear Miss Robins.

I hear from Mrs Clifford all the good in the world of your new creation — and I want greatly to give you a hand and to congratulate you on your new success. I gather — in this remote backwater, of the Grand Canal — that last Saturday night was an occasion very honourable to every one concerned, and that you had some superior chances and rose as high as the waters would float you. I am heartily glad of it. It's hateful to me to have but this faint echo — but I hope for more reverberations. Above all I hope that you are launched on a deep full tide. I wonder whether you will have time — after a bit — to tell me a word about the prospective future of the play? I've no personal news, and it's an insult, I feel, to incarcerated Londoners, to talk to them about gondolas and sunsets. But please be sure I am with you in yearnings of spirit. How I should like to send my blessing to Mrs Bell! But if one may neither give her to read nor expect her to write — ! Kindly tell her when you have a chance, of my message.

Yours, dear Miss Robins, devotedly,

Henry James

## CHAPTER VIII

# LITTLE EYOLF AND GUY DOMVILLE

'The first volume of my play book' is his 1894 'Theatricals.'

The implied question in: 'I wonder what you are doing' has its power to stir regret, for I am sorry, now, I did not tell Henry James my guilty secret. I was trying to learn to write fiction.

I was not doing this out of love for the art. Mr. James might indeed have cast that fact into the scale of his sanction. Certainly, he would in the end have sympathized with motives that weighed so heavily with me.

About the time of my Wyndham experience I had come to realize fully that the position of leading lady in an Actor-Manager's Theatre was not 'enough,' would never again be enough. Perhaps, as Wyndham said, I had been spoilt. My brief experiences of having a theatre, and a company of my own, had taught me a number of things. In 'leading lady' leading-strings I found the long fascination of the Theatre wearing thin.

When it became clear that independence could be achieved by another means, I was deeply thankful and mightily amused. For I would still be playing a part. Two short novels and the short stories of that time were published under a pseudonym, taken without exception to conceal the identity of a man.

I used to hear people speculating, attaching now this, now that established name to my inventions. About one of those little books of mine there was plenty of disagreement. When people at dinner parties praised it, I picked flaws. When they damned it, I defended, with an air successfully impersonal. It was immense fun.

I never in all this felt the smallest temptation to compromise my friendship with Henry James by making him a party to my indiscretions. I now think he would have recognized and treated gently my original impulse — too stoutly maintained — to spare him the necessity of making the effort to rescue me from an exhibition of blind audacity. Here was a young woman committed to the exercise of an arduous and exacting Art. And now, when a certain standing was won, she was for challenging fate on another field!! — that spectacle he must be spared.

## LVIII

*Grand Hotel,*
*Rome.*
June 2nd. ['94.]

Dear Miss Robins.

I have succeeded in getting time to thank you for your last good letter only by bolting from Venice, where 'people' were many, bless them, and quiet hours a perpetual massacre of the innocents. I mean the quiet hours themselves were perpetually put to the sword. So I have fled to the Eternal City on purpose to re-establish communication with you.

Rome is delightfully empty — save of 'Blanche Roosevelt'! — now, and still delightfully cool, with all sorts of unspeakable early-summer secrets and charms. There is even yet, in spite of all the horrors perpetrated these 15 years, no place on earth half so dear. I wish you would come and act here, as the Duse does in London!

Very interesting indeed to me was the letter enclosed in your note — the one of April 15th about Mrs Lessingham, its prospects and its melancholies. I can't help being glad I wasn't there — to be but the more dismally conscious of these. I enter with much emotion into all you say and feel even that you say it only too charitably. The vile Scott's vileness was sufficiently to be expected — but I'm bound to say I think —— fell below what one had a right to look to from him, even without looking for very much. And —— is one of the best — the only 'best' indeed! It must all have been sickening enough to you — and I'm afraid the whole episode hasn't contained many elements of joy. I can't write of it — in this comparatively 'distinguished' place — it all seems too ugly and too mean. But that only makes me want the more to be in the green chair again — where redeeming ideas and inglorious consolations may pass between us more quickly. Please believe with what satisfaction I shall occupy it on the first opportunity. That won't be very soon, indeed — as I shall scarcely be back in England before August 1st. How many things, however, I shall like to talk with you about then! Even here I do sneakingly wonder about some of them. Is the dreary 'Money' a success, for instance, and is Mrs Bancroft's niggerminstrelsy again making a fortune? I ask you this — but don't mind: I don't want, after all, an affirmative however veracious! I think I want a little more to hear if —— is only relatively, or quite positively, a failure in Jones's play — and if you've seen the latter? If she *is* a failure what was the meaning, or verity, of all the exaltation of her 'art' and talent and charm in the other thing? Such qualities, when an actress has them, don't pop in and out of holes, (out of parts) like mice! But you will tell me all about this — over a glass of vermouth. I consume quantities of that fluid here and never without thinking of you. When I do I wonder what you are 'doing'— with what seems to me such an odious out-of-the-bill-ness as 'Money' has brought about. I sent you a copy of the 1st Vol. of my play-book, the other day, to beguile your leisure; but they are things — the little pieces that you, alas, already know — I have published them only from an irresistible melancholy impulse to try and save so much extreme ingenuity (such as it is — for they all four cost me great labour and much time,) from 'dying with all their music in them',— I mean going down into utter silence and darkness. And also from a vulgarer motive — which the publisher knows. Mrs Bell sent me an invitation to a ball — and I thought of wiring you (certain you'd be there) for all the Waltzes. Then I knew you'd be taken — otherwise I should have come back for it. I pray that dear lady be better, and always kind to you, and not frustrated in fiction. I watch for her novel — though English novels, on the Continent, require much faith. I have just found mine terribly inadequate to the last volume of 'Marcella'! Do write me something good and strange and comfortable! and believe, dear Miss Robins, in the constant sympathy of yours most truly

Henry James

P.S.   34 De Vere Gardens, W. is always the best address for me.

Mrs. F. W. H. Myers's plan for my visiting Cambridge included, I think, playing Ibsen there. 'The enchanting French girl' was Mlle Thierry de la Noue.

## LIX

Monday.<br>[?July, 1894]

Dear Miss Robins.

It takes all my heroism to resist the note of exquisite invitation in your beautiful voice; but I grieve unfeignedly to say that it is impossible I should go to Redcar. My reasons are quite massive in their multiplicity — my hindrances are insuperable. Woe is me that I should say No to a combination of charming women. What a horrible place is the world which puts one to such shames. I *might* be able to go and see you at Cambridge — there! Doesn't that settle the question of your accepting Mrs Myers's invitation for you? All the other omens too seem to me to point to your doing so. I have never but one perfectly straight and simple precept: Act, *act,* ACT — whenever you can. I believe in your doing it exactly as I believe in a singer's practising her scales. But I *am* sorry we have to converse on the matter across the long dun wolds — I mean across all England. I don't care a bit for the enchanting French girl — and, though the dreadful waters of London are already closing over my head, I miss too much the enchanting Anglaise and the enchanting American. I reiterate my regrets and beg you to repeat them to Mrs Bell.

Do go to Cambridge — and let me know when!

The Autumn again brought in my way matter worthy of Mr. James's attention. The first sheets of Ibsen's 'Little Eyolf' had come. As soon as the translation was printed a set was sent to Mr. James.

## LX

Nov. 22nd, 1894

Dear Miss Robins.

Heinemann has lent me the proofs of the 2 first acts of the Play — the ineffable Play — and I can't stay my hand from waving wildly to you! It is indeed immense,— indeed and indeed. It is of rare perfection — and if 3 keeps up the tremendous pitch of 1 and 2 it will distinctly stand at the tiptop of his achievement. It's a masterpiece and a marvel; and it *must* leap upon the stage. It must leap with *your* legs, moreover — excuse, in an Ibsen connection, the metaphor! The inherent difficulties are there, but they are not insurmountable. They are on the contrary manageable — they are a matter of tact and emphasis — of art and discretion. The thing will be a big *profane* (i.e. Ibsen and non-Ibsen *both*) success. The part — *the* part is Asta — unless it be the Rat-hound in the Bag! *What* an old woman — and what a Young! — I am to see Mrs Bell to-day — but it isn't with her I want to talk of it, but with *you,* when I have gulped Act III.

Yours in convulsions

Henry James

While I laugh, a feeling of grateful astonishment goes out after the long interval as it must have gone when the unflinching verdicts of the next letter reached me first; gratitude for his rare and all the more impressive enthusiasm over the incomparable First Act of 'Little Eyolf,' and gratitude for that fresh proof of 'caring,' his anger and condemnation at the ending of the play — little as I agreed, or can to-day agree, with him. Some of the delight comes back, even a touch of the old triumph at his revulsion of feeling: 'You will think I am taking back my disappointment.' It was a revulsion, none the less, that left him confessing 'the beauty of the conversation — inconstestably exquisite,' and that led him on to submit to that ruling passion, sure sign in Henry James that the thing had seized him — the need to re-do it 'his way.' And yet how frankly he yielded to the Spirit of Place: 'the gathered northern twilight, the flag down, the lights coming out across the fjord;' and most significant of all, his conviction that he could see in the final scene, implications tragic, poetic, which had escaped the painter of it!

All this was fresh proof of the power in the old magician that could so ignite the wary alien mind.

## LXI

*34 De Vere Gardens, W.*
November 25th [1894]

Dear Miss Robins.

I am horrified at having appeared to you to have been indiscreet about the play, — I think it must have been through Mrs Green that I so appeared — as it was to the sole Mrs Green, in the despair of a dull dinner — or after-dinner — at Sir Alfred Lyall's, that I murmured a few intensely sketchy words into the ear of, with a general sense that I was exciting curiosity, and working toward a boom, rather than anything else — with a general vague sense, too, that *she* would probably be in your confidence. But the fewer communicants, certainly, the better — and you may be sure that I shan't breathe a syllable to anyone else. I can't think of another person to whom I *have* breathed — and if I had got the 2 acts direct from yourself I probably shouldn't have spoken even to Mrs G. Receiving them so freely from Heinemann, without a word of caution, I was no doubt unduly off my guard. But as *you* probably cautioned Mrs G., no harm will have been done — and shan't be. I fear, in truth, no harm *can* be done equal to the harm done to the play by its own most disappointing third act. It came to me last night — and has been, to me, a subject of depressed reflection. It seems to me a singular and almost inexplicable drop — dramatically, *representably* speaking; in short strangely and painfully meagre. It has beauty, as you say — but only as far as anything so meagre *can* have it. The worst of it is that it goes back, as it were, on what precedes, and gives a meagreness to that too — makes it less interesting and less significant. He simplifies too much and too suddenly. It doesn't surprise me, indeed — for one had the sense that with his paucity of elements, of figures, he had, in 1 and 2, squeezed out of these things every drop that they would yield; still, at the same time, one dimly expected a sort of miracle — based on the fact that Act 2 carried on the action of Act I. more than could have been hoped. I don't see the meaning or effect of Borgheim — I don't see the value or final *function* of Asta; that is, I don't in the *presentation* of these things — that it's the presentation that constitutes the play. On the other hand the beauty of the conversations between Allmers and Rita is incontestably even exquisite — and I even think it will give you, or would give you, a great deal to do with Rita. My objection is that I find the solution too simple, too immediate, too much a harking back, and too productive of the sense that there might have been a stronger one. I have just paused to read it over again, and the effect of doing so is to make me feel that an *actress* no doubt (i.e. E. R.) could do an immense deal with Rita. My idea that Asta was to become an active, *the* active, agent is of course blighted. Really uttered, *done,* in the gathered northern twilight, with the flag blown and the lights coming out across the fjord, the scene might have a real solemnity of beauty — and perhaps that's all that's required!! — A vulgar material drawback seems to me the shortness — inadequate duration — of the whole thing — and in especial the brevity of this last, reduced to the 2 simple conversations. Still the second conversation *is* lovely: oh yes, it is. You will think I am taking back my 'disappointment'! I am not; it is perfectly consistent with my appreciation. The talk between husband and wife is charming — but one listens to it as if it had been a substitute for something else to which one suspects it of being inferior. But the audience may quite possibly prefer the substitute. — On the question of you yourself taking responsibility in the matter I feel very powerless to advise you. Much as I should like to see the play done here, 3rd act and all, I understand but too well that you should shrink from taking the enterprise on your shoulders — that it should seem to you too great a load and a strain. It would require huge courage. Too discouraging seems the situation in which, in such a case, that barbarous solution is the only one. But *is* it the only one? — is there absolutely no one in London with a theatre and a *mind?* I think them over and I confess I see no beckoning portal. I fear Allmers will never be thought an actor manager's part. But all this may clarify as you go. I should like to talk of it with you — instead of this barren writing — but I shall have to wait for your return. I'm sorry to say Manchester is impossible to me. May it prove magnificently possible to *you!* I fear I shall know nothing till I see you again — but I pray your cup overflow with the wine of success and the notes of the Bank of England. My love to Mrs Bell!

Yours always<br>Henry James

Mrs. Hugh Bell and I were coming down from Yorkshire to be present at his premiére of 'Guy Domville.'

## LXII

Dear Mrs Bell.

You are both heroic and angelic — the one in your benevolence the other in your activity. I blush for what you propose to do for me — but it is partly with conscious pride. Soyez tranquille, Madame — you shall of course have your stall — and from the author's trembling hand; and Miss Robins shall have hers, and they shall be snugly side by side. Don't trouble about the box office — or if you have already written, repose in peace: the seats will come to you from me, and you have nothing more to do. It is a great bleak feat for you to achieve — may you not feel yourself too utterly swindled! We will talk of all things then, and I will tell you indeed how Hugo, on the winter evenings, lights up the dusky anteroom of Eton Chapel with his quite heavenly presence. It is a joy to behold him. A bientôt. Yours in great haste ever        Henry James

P.S. Since I wrote this — 2 hours ago — has come the unspeakable news of R. L. S.'s death. I am too sickened to speak of it — it's a desolation!

On the last night of the Old Year, he wrote, about 'Guy Domville'— due at the St. James's on January 5th — this very human and touching letter.

## LXIII

*34 De Vere Gardens, W.*
Monday.
[Dec. 31, 1894]

My Dear Elizabeth Robins.

Something deep and strange within me tells me that your letter is a really good omen; and for a moment it stills the quite ridiculous frenzy of my nervous pulses. All thanks then for it — from a heart which devoutly echoes your invocation. No one — not even Mrs Bell (please tell her) can wish for me more than I wish for myself! The portents, on the whole, I think, are as good as they can be — or as I can *read* them — in the case of a thing as to which I now mainly feel that it *has* been abbreviated and simplified out of all *close* resemblance to my intention. I have worked and participated with unremitting zeal and intensity — and my afflicted consciousness has been divided between desolation at the immensity of my sacrifices (of things — touches, passages, details — indispensable to real interest and coherence) and exultation over the very absence of things not left in the piece for them *not* to do! The bare minimum (excuse my awful writing) is at once so much the worse and so much the better for my play! Not that they are not, poor dears, doing their zealous best. There is *one* actor in the affair, little Esmond and remarkably clever and capable, a (on usual and obvious but most sensible lines) quite *masterly* stage-manager — I mean of course G. A. [George Alexander]. They have all been most comfortable and decorous, and the rehearsals very human and tranquil — I mean without 'incidents.' As for the poor little play itself, aching in every fibre from its wounds and — valeat quantum: which means 'I shall do the next time so much better.' It will be a very creditable performance, and a very finished production. Only I feel more and more that I *may* be made for the Drama (God only knows!) but am not made for the Theatre! I rejoice more than I can say in the plain ivory Satin Duchess 'pikestaff.' I hope Mrs Bell will be equally ascetic. I am told that I shall receive the tickets for your stall and Mrs Bell's to-day — to send them to you myself — so they will come to you to-morrow or Wednesday — and Mrs Clifford is, I believe to be alongside of you.

I am sorry to say there is a bad (theatrical) *wind* rising — which is always a worry: that is, Grundy's play at the Garrick is described to me on several sides as a hopeless failure — and the wretched papers this a.m. seem to really say as much. I have a superstitious sense that such influences are contagious. Still, contagion means contact, and I can't say I do think there are many points of contact between

'Slaves of the Ring' as I hear (and see) it confoundingly described and my little clutch at lucidity. Poor Miss Calhoun — I am told her part is impossible, but her art excellent. Bless the Barns! * Yours in all gratitude

Henry James

## LXIV

*34 De Vere Gardens, W.*

Dear Mrs Bell.

Forgive the uncontrollable accident if you have received from the box office of the theatre a stall you will have had to pay for, instead of receiving it from my hand and gratis, as I showily promised you. It will take too long for me to explain this complication — I will do so later viva voce. The tension at the box office is too fearful for me to alter anything. I posted Miss Robins her stall this a.m., chez vous and I trust it will safely have reached her. A bientôt chère Madame. The dew of agony is already on my brow; and the idea of your travelling so far for si peu de chose haunts the fevered slumbers of yours, dear Mrs Bell, apologetically

Henry James

P.S. Je vous la souhaite bien bonne!
Jan. 1st, 1895.

There were moments when Mr. James's friends felt they had suffered more than he over the

* The Hugh Bell's Yorkshire House, Red Barns.

strange fate of 'Guy Domville.' For he had at
least the stern comfort of bearing himself in
an unprecedented crisis with an unprecedented
candour and dignity.

It was true that Mr. James *was* made for the
drama and not, under the given conditions, for
the Theatre. It meant more than he probably
ever knew, that under those particular conditions
'Guy Domville' had the success with the discrimi-
nating that it did have.

Of the leading dramatic critics, William Archer
and Bernard Shaw were the only ones whose
opinion reverberated with any real authority.

William Archer wrote:

> 'Since "Beau Austin," we have seen nothing on
> the English stage so charming as the first act of
> "Guy Domville." The motives are delicately inter-
> woven, yet remain clear and convincing; the scenes
> are ordered with a master-hand and the writing is
> graceful without mannerism.'

Mr. Archer then went on to point out 'one slight
mistake' or rather one missed opportunity, and
so into a general discussion.

Bernard Shaw in the course of one of his criti-
cisms best worth reading again, begins by quoting
'the drama's laws the drama's patrons give.' 'Pray
which of its patrons? — the cultivated majority
who, like myself and all the ablest of my col-
leagues, applauded Mr. James on Saturday, or
the handful of rowdies who brawled at him? It
is the business of the dramatic critic to educate
these dunces, not to echo them.

'Admitting, then, that Mr. James's dramatic
authorship is valid, and that his plays are du
théâtre when the right people are in the theatre,

164

what are the qualities and faults of "Guy Domville"? First among the qualities, a rare charm of
speech. Line after line comes with such a delicate
turn and fall that I unhesitatingly challenge any
of our popular dramatists to write a scene in verse
with half the beauty of Mr. James's prose. I am
not now speaking of the verbal fitness, which is
a matter of careful workmanship merely. I am
speaking of the delicate inflexions of feeling conveyed by the cadences of the line, inflexions and
cadences which, after so long a course of the ordinary theatrical splashes and daubs of passion and
emphasis are as grateful to my ear as the music
of Mozart's "Entführung aus dem Serail" would
be after a year of "Ernani" and "Il Trovatore."
Second, "Guy Domville" is a story, and not a
mere situation hung on a gallows of plot. And it
is a story of fine sentiment and delicate manners,
with an entirely worthy and touching ending.
Third, it relies on the performers, not for the
brute force of their personalities and popularities,
but for their finest accomplishments in grace of
manner, delicacy of diction and dignity of style. . .
It will be a deplorable misfortune if "Guy Domville" does not hold the stage long enough to
justify Mr. Alexander's enterprise in produc-
ing it.'

The man of whom such things can be written
by one of the most acute minds living might have
served the theatre well.

My own feeling is that, had Mr. James given
himself to it twenty-five years earlier, the theatre
would have rewarded him. For the theatre is a
place where you must first learn, before you can
fitly practise.

## LXV

*34 De Vere Gardens, W.*
Thursday.
[Jan. 10, 1895]

Dear Miss Robins.

I will come in some night next week — with pleasure — letting you know well in advance. I have mainly, for this immediate time, an intense desire to be intensely *still* — a want of rest; as I now find, am finding, how excessively tired I got with those five weeks of high-pressure rehearsals.

I know nothing whatever of how 'G.D.' is going — not having been near the theatre since Monday night — at which I assisted from the gallery (where they were *lovely*,) and which, before a remarkably good house, went like an enthusiastic and brilliant 1st. This, however, was the inevitable swing of the 1st night's devilish pendulum — into the other sense; and I don't make too much of it. I only live — as regards the piece, from day to day, and am wholly prepared for the worst. I have got the whole thing wonderfully behind me and below me — at any rate away from me. — The paragraph in the *Westminster* represents, I believe, an impression on the part of many *observers* of the first night who were in various parts of the theatre, who got a sense of predetermined mischief, and of incongruities and anomalies in the composition, aspect and attitude of the gallery, of which symptoms were early perceptible

&c. But I know nothing about the matter, nor do I in the least care.

G. A. showed me (the 1st thing — on Sat. night) his telegram, which he found, on Monday, by inquiry at the Sloane St. P.O., where it had caused, on being handed in there, on Sat. p.m., much excitement. that it had been left by two ladies. He wondered, I think, if there were not a connection between the two phenomena — but may now be quite of the opinion there was none. It is all too base and ugly and obscure. I hope you are seeing *your* way. Ever yours

Henry James.

## LXVI

*34 De Vere Gardens, W.*
Saturday.

Dear Miss Robins.

I have never thanked you for your kind letter of Sunday last — about the late 'G.D.' availing myself of your suggestion that I shouldn't — because it has been a week of much occupation with many things — as well as of very numb fingers. But all thanks, at any rate, to-day. It has been a great relief to feel that one of the most detestable incidents of my life has closed. It has left me with an unutterable horror of the theatre — as well as with a blank uncertainty as to what that horror — bearing on everything that relates to it — will lead me to do in regard to the same — to it, for it, at it, against it! However, whatever this may be doesn't at present matter, as all such doings will be long remotely distant. The sense of that distance is my own comfort — but the gulf isn't too wide to prevent my wishing you all satisfaction in what you may yourself be planning or achieving. Indeed I shall take you as a remedy — a soothing potion — as you are poured out and administered. I hope you have a nice thick layer of snow on the roof of your flat to keep you warm. I can't think of anything else that seems to me to meet the case. It is not, however I trust so bad as mine, who insanely go out of town this p.m. for a Saturday to Monday visit — contracted for — a 100 years ago — on a muggy day. You see there is no time you *don't* have to pray for yours, dear Miss Robins, always

Henry James

There was a general impression that Mr. James was much beset by the attentions of ladies. One story dates from the days when domestic electric lighting was not yet fully under control. The first of the great London establishments to install the new luxury was, if I remember, Grosvenor House. At the subsequent evening party when the scene was at its most brilliant, suddenly the lights went out. As suddenly they came on, to discover — so the story went — thirteen ladies clinging to Mr. James.

I had myself seen the sensation made by his appearance at a tea party, and realized to some extent the numbers of invitations and beseechments he had to parry. Some that pressed too hard he was capable of treating with a formidable irony. But in spite of being so sought, entreated, 'claimed,' he retained with an endearing freshness his appreciation for the little courtesies of friendship and affection.

'95' was the number of the Hugh Bells' house in Sloane Street.

## LXVII

Dear Mrs Bell.

It was impossible yesterday afternoon — it was impossible. I hoped against hope, till the 11th hour — but was obliged, to my great regret to succumb to the sternness of the situation and recognize how far I have gone in committing myself — none too soon — to utterly renouncing and abjuring the afternoon teaparty. It has been a cruel and most surgical operation — but I have had to extirpate utterly the peccant humours which lead to such occasions. I have lopped off the erratic limb and, though mutilated and disfigured, am — comme qui dirait — *saved*. To lose myself — to *damn* myself — again for 95 (I don't allude, though I might, to the number of the ladies) was, for a critical hour yesterday, a tremendous temptation — but I spent the hour in fervent prayer. — The tête-à-tête I cling to more fondly than ever, as I shall soon exhibit to you again. — No doubt you are right as regards Miss E., and advice and the future and all the rest of it. In

169

fact I think this was the attitude I originally confessed to you on my own. She will 'come out all
right.' So shall I, dear Mrs Bell — if cautious about
the 95. (That is an allusion to the no. of the ladies.)
Yours most faithfully and shyly

Henry James.

The 'three volumes' in the letter following refers to Mrs. Hugh Bell's novel 'The Story of
Ursula.'

## LXVIII

*34 De Vere Gardens, W.*
April 23rd [1895]

Dear Mrs Bell.

It will seem to you preposterous that this should
be the answer to your gracious little birthday word
— of so many days ago — but such is the improbable
fact, which you and I would never venture (would
we?) to interweave into one of our fictions. I was
born, afresh, on April 15th, into impediments
innumerable and it isn't till this very instant that I
have worked them off. Meanwhile your little pic-
tured symbol of sympathy has sustained and re-
freshed my lonely labour. It was charming of you
to send it. It was one of my two birthday presents —
I had none others. The second was a visit from Miss
Robins — as I sat by my fire meekly enduring a
horrid sore throat, in the cultivation of which I

spent my whole incarcerated Eastertide. This was the blessing — the graceful apparition — that you can easily figure. A quand the graceful apparition of Mrs Bell? 'The summer comes, with flowers and bee' (as I used to learn in infancy) but you are distinctly 'backward.' I expect wonders when you do come. I am counting the hours till Mrs. Clifford lends me, as she has promised, three palpitating volumes. Then you may expect wonders from *me*. I don't subscribe, but I usually buy. This year is so bad with me, however, that I am almost reduced to stealing. On se l'arrache. Let me repeat how much I wish you would *arrash* — autre souvenir d'enfance — *yourself* from those who inconsiderately detain you là bas.

Yours, and ever theirs, dear Mrs Bell, always

Henry James

## CHAPTER IX

# MARIANA

Our 1895 play-going took us to Duse, Sarah, and I think, Réjane. Certainly it included that evening dedicated to the Theatre when Mr. James came to read me his Ellen Terry play.

In a letter written to his brother in December 1893: 'I have come to hate the whole theatrical subject,' he said. But he never hated it, except in the passionate reaction of his love for it.

And so, there was presented a curious spectacle. Though he had abjured the theatre with such violence, here he was, only a few months after 'Guy Domville,' and after writing to his brother about the 'horror' bred of that experience '... I feel as if the simple freedom of mind thus begotten, to return to one's legitimate form, would be simply by itself a divine solace for everything'— here was the master of fiction still ready, if not eager, to give himself to the theatre, while the actress was giving herself less and less, and for the rest was sipping in secret at Mr. James's 'divine' cup.

He naturally often talked about novels, and very freely as time went on about novel-writing

— for one reason, because so many of our friends were 'at it.' At first his verdicts would astonish me. I saw many of my own and other people's idols in the dust. Again it was the French who found the nearest approach to favour. Despair would settle on him when he recalled the gift of a book from this or that English novelist. He positively could not, he said, read anything, now, for sake of the story. He had 'lost his innocence.' If a book interested him he wanted to rewrite it.

The most moderate intelligence in his interlocutor might have led her to catch at the rich possibility of learning something about novel-writing from so priceless a lesson as seeing some of her sentences rewritten by Henry James. But apart from the justified conviction that an actress would find fair treatment from Press and public only through strict anonymity — to be rewritten was not what I wanted. I think I saw dimly, but felt acutely, that form and content are difficult to divorce. My business, as by the light of hope I saw it, was to seize on certain phases as they appeared to my eyes and draw them as *true* as my kind of vision would let me, and keep them true to that vision; above all, keep them as alive as I could contrive.

In any case Mr. James had to prosecute his highly finished work. I had my highly unfinished — my never to be finished — work; and in that spirit I sat down to my first long novel. In the years that followed if Mr. James, who had generously given me so many of his own books, was never offered novel or story of mine, this Offering of Abstention was my way of showing how much

173

I cared for his peace, and how very much for his unanxious friendship.

But a play was another matter altogether. In the first year of our acquaintance, with an inscription on the fly-leaf of the 'Tragic Muse' he did for me what he desired — warmed and flattered, without at all misleading me. For even at that early day I *was* his 'friend'; I might truly be, as he wrote, his 'colleague' in those labours and hopes that had the theatre for their goal. It will make clearer my sense of the ease and pleasure of the 'play-approach,' as distinguished from the novel, to say that I never once from the beginning to the end, hesitated in any stage-project to ask, and to receive, his interest and a liberal share of his most precious time.

Of the two outstanding instances 'Mariana' falls in this year of 1895. A Four Act romantic drama by the Spaniard José Echegaray had, so it was said, been tampered with and thrown into a kind of English which those who knew Spanish declared was not even literally faithful, and which I knew would be unspeakable on the stage. Since I couldn't read Spanish, one of my friends, to show me — not the poetic beauty of 'Mariana' (he was afraid *that* might be untranslatable) — but just to give me an idea of the dramatic fire and force of the play, undertook to make in all haste a perfectly bald literal translation, to serve as a foundation that I might work on later.

All this being done and the new version, as much as might be, licked into shape, it was put before Mr. James.

## LXIX

*34 De Vere Gardens, W.*

Dear Miss Robins.

I am much moved in thinking over our reading of last night to reasseverate, with the force that comes from a more deliberate judgment, my strong sense of the great omens that cluster about 'Mariana.' It seems to me, as I turn it round in my mind, a very fine thing — a very valuable thing. It is worth all your effort and all your patience. Put them forth and you will conquer. Do the very best for it you can. It is only the best that will be any good for it. That 4th Act is magnificent and the thing lives in one's mind. It is a very strong little drama — *and an immense* chance for you. Above all I want to repeat that any hand I can lend to help the matter, the version, the text, the actability, will be joyfully bestowed by yours always

Henry James

Sunday p.m.

## LXX

*34 De Vere Gardens, W.*
Friday p.m.

Dear Miss Robins.

I am delighted to hear of your completely secured contract, and I shall be delighted to give 'Mariana' as many hours as she may require. But this evening is bad, alas, for I am having 3 men to dinner at a Club, and they will stay till impossibly late. *Next week* I could give a goodish bit of time — preferably *evenings*. Would *Wednesday and Thursday, 25th and 26th* suit you to begin with? I would come to Dorset St. at any hour you say; even by 8.30. Then we could arrange for more time. I am sorry about to-night. I *could* manage Sunday p.m. (after dinner) Monday 23rd I dine out; and Tuesday is rather bad for me. But I have also Saturday 28th at your service. But let us begin Wednesday — ?

Yours in great haste
Henry James

He was taken at his word. Evening after evening he would sit with that sustained patience, discussing, mending, polishing. Usually he would dictate and I would set down. Now and then he would pull out his gold pencil and then leave it dangling before some intractable difficulty. Or, sheer excitement kindled by that most entrancing play in the world, the Game of Words, would bring him to his feet. He would pace the little space between fire and bookcase, one act of the type-script in hand, making passes in the air, and with: 'No, no, dear lady,' sweep my suggestion out of his way and in the cleared space plant some final flower of grace or fitness.

The hunt for the real right epithet would go on sometimes till I, weakly ready to abandon it, would be brought to my senses by his suddenly dealing himself a resounding smack on the forehead, and I would see the open palm flung out to

Luisa     (Laughing)

          Why, you are at the most ~~fascinating~~ time of life.

Phil.     How good of you to say so, Donna Luisa.  I shall beg your

          brother's permission to offer you my hand and heart.

Clara     In the meantime, let us return to Mariana.

Phil.     Then you hadn't quite made an end of her?

Clara     No, indeed; .there's a great deal more to be said about

          the ~~enchanting~~ *memberable* widow.

Luisa     Widow  I don't think she ought to be called a widow.  You

          know her father married her by ~~proxy~~ *proxy* to her Mexican *millionaire*

          ~~millionaire~~ *as if she had been a jowness, but* ~~and~~ when she got to America, she found only

          *So you can't say she's quite a wife* the dead body of her husband awaiting her.  ~~And, frankly~~

          *a wife or proper. Can you call such a woman a wid.*

Clara / Louisa   (to Don Philip) ~~Ought she to rank as a widow~~ *a woman a wid.*

          *You might call her a widow on paper.*

Phil.     ~~Well, suppose we call her a widow by proxy.  That cannot~~

          ~~be said of you, Donna Luisa.~~ *That's not the sort you are, Doña Luisa.*

Luisa     No, ~~sir~~.  Poor Parco!

Phil.     *Nor you* ~~nor of you~~, Donna Clara.

Clara     Of me?  Why, I'm not any sort of widow.  Have you for-

          gotten Castulo?

Phil.     True!  true!  what a head I have!- Castulo!  the high

          priest of archæology!  Ha; talk of angels -

Clara     Here he comes with Luciano - poor boy!

Phil.     What ~~supplicating~~ *entreaty* looks ~~the poor lad sends to you~~, Donna

          Clara - won't you rescue him?

Clara     Why should I?  Castulo is improving his mind.

Phil.     Do throw him a lifebuoy.

SOME OF MR. JAMES'S CORRECTIONS IN THE TYPESCRIPT OF
ECHEGARAY'S *Mariana*

hold up 'as it were' the found solution for the benediction of heaven. Of the several copies of 'Mariana' the dustiest shows that Mr. James did not always leave the scrivener's part to me. The marks of his hand, scattered through the typescript, brings back the very roll of his voice, substituting 'my dear lady' for Donna Luisa, 'incomparable' for enchanting widow, and instead of feminine delicacy and masculine strength: 'smooth as your sex and hard as mine,' in the unmistakable James handwriting.

## LXXI

*34 De Vere Gardens, W.*
Sunday

Dear Miss Robins.

I will come on Tuesday p.m. at *9,* and wait for you if you're not back. Don't think me the most insecure of men if I then propose, probably, after all, a substitute for Thursday 26th (for reasons I will tell you.) I have, thank God, almost all evenings free *next* week — 29th, 30th, 1st, 2nd, 3rd, &c., &c.

Yours ever

Henry James


'Mariana,' was not to be produced till after Christmas, but this was the year when I began to be a great deal at the Edward Greys' Fishing Cottage in Hampshire. I came back from Itchen Abbas to engage the company and arrange rehearsals for Ibsen's 'Little Eyolf.'

## LXXII

*34 De Vere Gardens, W.*
March 6th [1896]

Dear Miss Robins.

I am horrified and bewildered by your note. 'Forgotten' *what* — forgotten when? I haven't the smallest recollection of our having parted last on an understanding about *Thursday* — but on an understanding, on the contrary, that you would *let me know after Monday* (the day you were to read the Spaniard to Comyns Carr, wasn't it?) some hour and day that *would* suit you. So I have hoped each day for a word from you, only abstaining from sending you one of reminder, because I have been utterly driven and goaded with work — and everything else — and thought you probably were also much preoccupied. Squeeze and shake my memory as I will, it doesn't yield me a faint echo of any word between us subsequent to that fragment of dialogue (at Mrs Boughton's) about my *waiting* for a sign from you. So that if I did forget (and *you* are not deluded) my memory is indeed a void almost alarming for its necessary working. I am at any rate horribly grieved that you sat vainly waiting there for me — we seem nowadays to have nothing but cross-purposes and a [illegible] of hindrance. But I don't mean to give up or let you go — and I will pursue you to the death.

To-night there is another impossibility — I take Mrs Jekyll (a promise 3 months old to take her to

178

the theatre) to see 'Shamus O'Brien.' So it goes. But won't you *some night next week — any* save Monday — *to be fixed in writing by yourself* go with me to see something — dining with me for the purpose first? Or if there is nothing fit to be seen, will you dine without going? However, the going will be better — if you will for instance risk the COMEDY. I had a visit yesterday from Miss Calhoun and promised her I would, if possible, see her. I shall wire you in the a.m. to ask if you will go to Miss Bateman's recital with me at 3. With renewed grief, bewilderment and blankness about our fiasco yesterday.

Yours, dear Miss Robins, pertinaciously

Henry James

'Little Eyolf' was produced at the Avenue Theatre on November 23rd, 1896.

Mr. James, if I remember, was doing some re-furnishing about this time. He found there were certain things that he now had no place for. 'The elephantine object' referred to, was the chair which, along with a couple of ancient mirrors (one a Queen Anne, the other an Adam) have ever since been among my cherished possessions.

# LXXIII

Dear Miss Robins.

I accept with joy and gratitude the box for the 1st performance: it will be an immense pleasure to occupy it.

I have forborne to write to you ever since I got, ten days ago or more, a little word from you: for the reason that I knew you to be overwhelmed with labour and worry and it was common humanity to let you alone. But there has been one thing I've wanted much to say — only it can (it *must*) wait till after 'Little E.' Don't you want something *more* done to 'Mariana'? I am eagerly and entirely at your service and whenever that day comes only let me know — *then*. We left her, last, susceptible of such improvement! I am sure we can help her further. I needn't say how I pray for the present job. How immersed you must be — and how tired! But I don't see how your bill can be anything but a huge draw — it *must* pull like 'wild horses.' I felt that from the *mere* look of it at the door of the Avenue as I passed there yesterday. I have here, waiting, the elephantine object (the chair,) you kindly said you will relieve me of; but its presence is a complication I won't add to your existence till after Production, but perhaps meanwhile I may find means to cut it down so that it may get into your door or window.

Yours with the fondest participation

Henry James

It is good to remember that Mr. James did not feel his labour on 'Mariana' wasted. He was glad that play should be the means of bringing to the actress the best 'notice' ever vouchsafed her by the stiffest dramatic critic of the time, William Archer. The play itself and, very particularly, the translation were greatly praised. It was like Mr. James, as the person so largely responsible for this last, to be entirely content that no name but that of the original translator (from whom I had secured the rights) should appear on the programme and in the Press.

Though out of place chronologically, No. LXXIV puts a seal on 'Mariana' that I should be sorry to see detached.

## LXXIV

*Lamb House,*
*Rye, Sussex.*
October 14th, 1903

My dear Elizabeth Robins.

Most happy and beautiful and touching to me the inspiration that dictated your letter, and striking that chord of the unforgotten past that ever, for me, vibrates with a force of which the pleasure is half pain — I mean the pain of intensity itself. It was a joy to me to see you again the other day and made me feel afresh what a wretched perpetual *missing* matter your absence is that is kept being at this end of it. Please believe that I now count it as a big precious lump in the good scale that these next months (of this exemplary season) are to have and to hold you. I shall be much more in London as the weeks go on. I am more touched than I can say by your allusion to that long stretch of time so tinged with the theatre, which I have often regarded and treated as a particular plot of retrospective frequentation of my own (almost) *only* — so that I have walked and sat in it rather, as one brooding and re-visiting alone. It will be delightful to walk there with *you,* one of these next times — when you will find that there is not an hour or an episode that doesn't still live for me. I think the Mariana hour is almost, perhaps, the most vivid and [illegible] — though each other easily becomes that as soon as I begin to focus it. Meantime it is as good (really!) as another pair of green and red chemists' jars shining into the dear old London autumn dusk, to know that a local habitation and a number holds you fast and that Lucy Clifford's beneficent hand adds to this reality of the fact. I can brush away Wheeling Virginia (was it Wheeling? *) which made me, the other day, uncannily, uneasy for the time. Your allusion to Duse makes me restless — I am too utterly busy and tied here this week and next to be able

* Winchester.

to see her, and yet I hate to lose her, and I chafe and groan. But we will talk of these things, and I am yours very constantly.

Henry James

After the Spanish play 'Mariana,' was to come the newest Ibsen: 'John Gabriel Borkman,' first referred to by Mr. James in a letter written while the 'Little Eyolf' Series was still going on at the Avenue Theatre.

## LXXV

*34 De Vere Gardens, W.*
Friday
Dec. 18, 1896

Dear Miss Robins.

I am coming to the Avenue to-night and hoping to see you once or twice in the entr'actes and even, if you can, to drive home with you — or, rather, to *drive* you home; and this is a word of warning to make my application at the Stage door more convenient to you. It is above all an overflow of my exaltation over the 1st 2 Acts of 'John-Gabriel' which I have just read in the French of the *Revue de Paris:* an exaltation prepared and confirmed by Mrs Green's telling me last night of your blessed possession of the play and preparedness to produce it. It is magnificent and Ella Rendheim *for* you from top to toe and floor to ceiling. She is a part to do *everything* with, a wondrous chance. *DO ask*

183

*Mrs Crowe to do Mrs Borkman.* It seems to me she's for *her,* too. Ah, who will 'do' J. —— Gabriel? He's immense. What an old boy is our Northern Henry! — he is too delightful — an old darling! The possible *when* &c., &c. are thrilling things you must tell me. I shall be, to-night, probably, in the 1st or 2nd row of stalls. I have let you alone with a severity worthy of a better cause — if there *were* a better than saving you any *extra* human strife and personal fatigue. But *do* try to see me to-night as much as possible — as Mrs G. tells me of your immediate flight to Redcar. There are a 100 things I wish to ask and to say — above all: Go it, Ella! I go to-morrow afternoon to see Tessa Gosse do Mr Puff in the 'Critic,' and in the evening to see Irving do — what he *does* do, alas, in 'Richard'! A bientôt:

Ever yours<br>Henry James

P.S. Tessa * in Mr Puff, is of course inspired by Sarah in 'Lorenzaccio!'


In writing about tickets for 'Mariana' (as though he owed *us* thanks, in face of all he had done for that play) Mr. James again stresses a point that he might be thought to take too seriously. In order to make clear to some extent the course of these small theatrical events and Mr. James's reaction to them, something must be said about the kind and the amount of work that was being done behind the scenes.

* Daughter of Mr. Edmund Gosse.

'Mariana' was the seventh of the plays for whose production I was mainly responsible. Those seven represented the harvest, such as it was, of hopes and plans indulged in so gaily, so confidently, by Marion Lea and me in 1890 and 1891. Little in quantity as had been done, the principle behind it was, I think, proved to the satisfaction of our own small public. It was proved at a cost that did not appear in our audited accounts.

Each new production meant, not as in regular theatres the carrying on of a business of which the framework remained the same, the machinery the same, the heads of Department and, most of all, the company the same. Each new play, given outside the established London managements, meant a new attack and a fresh campaign. It meant canvassing the field for a new theatre (the same one was seldom available) it meant the delicate, vital business of choosing a new cast; it meant 'working in' one's views of stage management often with a new stage-manager and (as a part of the general responsibility) trying to arrive at a business competence under circumstances where artistic competence and freedom to increase *that* should have been the main if not the sole concern.

It seems stranger to me now than it did at the time that what was involved in this outpouring of nervous energy should be understood by few, if any, so sensitively as by Henry James.

# LXXVI

Dear Miss Robins.

A thousand thanks for the so beautifully benevolent tickets for Friday. Besides being particularly welcome, they have the value of showing me that you are still in the breach and not — as I have been confidently expecting to hear — in your lonely, honoured grave. I hope with all my heart that you are finding strength — in Queen's Gate, if nowhere else. I have let you most reverently alone, and have been holding my breath — though also asking questions of all the Mrs Greens and Mrs Grosvenors. With little effect, however, for we have only mingled our prayers. These continue, on my part at least, violently, and I really think they must do you some good. To write so much — forgive me — isn't indeed to let you alone. Therefore I am only

Very gratefully yours

Henry James.

## CHAPTER X

# THE NEW CENTURY THEATRE

On May 3rd, 1897, 'John Gabriel Borkman'
was ushered in by a newly formed association
which had developed out of the Ibsen-Echegaray
(Little Eyolf-Mariana) ventures.

The work had been sustained and extended
through the unstinted labours of Mr. William
Archer. He had perhaps seen in the wild projects
of the Lea-Robins Joint Management, six years
before, possibilities of working out, in little, some
of the great problems that would confront the
National Theatre of his own dreams.

That this view of the matter gathered force appears in an article by A. B. Walkley on the prospectus of the little society that called itself at first
'The Minority' and later, with a largeness and
over-assurance that time was to chasten, 'The
New Century Theatre.' As I do not seem to have
kept a copy of the first leaflet I will borrow a part
of an account of it by the future dramatic critic
of *The Times*. After saying that the prospectus
'is a modest and business-like document,' Mr.
Walkley goes on:

187

[The New Century Theatre] 'does not regard itself as an end but as a means. "The sole endeavour of the executive will be to further the cause of Dramatic Art, and, without bias or prejudice, to pave the way for the permanent institution, artistically administered which is essential to the development of the drama and of acting." Presumably this permanent institution is to be an endowed theatre. If so, it will have to be privately endowed — for among the "new departures" which the next century is to give us I think we may be pretty confident that a State-aided English drama will not be included. There are a few enthusiasts among us — Mr. William Archer, I believe is one of them — who still have pleasant dreams of State-aid. Happy dreamers! ... what I chiefly like about the new enterprise is that it has no intention of being a happy-hunting-ground for the cranks. The executive "would have it clearly understood that they do not go in search of the esoteric, the eccentric, or the mystic; that they are devoted to no special school or tendency; that their productions will not be exclusively 'literary,' in the narrow sense of the word, and still less 'educational' or instructive; that they do not propose, in a word, to present the Undramatic Drama in any of its disguises. They will welcome all *acting plays,* of a certain standard of intrinsic merit, which are likely to interest the intelligent public to whom they appeal." The word "intelligent" here will cause the ungodly to blaspheme. Many angry gentlemen may safely be trusted to tell the New Century Theatre people that they are giving themselves airs of superior "intelligence." ... Fair-minded people, however, will recognize that there is really nothing arrogant, nothing aggressive, in the new scheme. "The aim of the executive is to provide a permanent machinery for

188

the production, from time to time, of plays of intrinsic interest which find no place on the stage in the ordinary way of theatrical business;" that is to say, their aim is not to rival but to supplement the ordinary theatres. They expressly disclaim any "spirit of antagonism towards the existing theatres. They recoginize cordially the artistic spirit displayed by many of the leading managers, from some of whom they have already received the most ungrudging assistance. Prevailing conditions, however, render the production of new pieces at the West-end theatres a matter of extreme costliness, and they leave no borderland between sensational success and disastrous failure. The aim of the Century Theatre is to raise the standard of merit in plays, while very largely lowering the standard of receipts required to constitute an honourable success." There is the real secret of the new scheme. It has an economic, quite as much as an artistic origin.'

It had been recognized that the success of a National Theatre would largely depend on the holder of the most important of the executive posts — that of Director. He must combine a genius for administration with a special flair for the theatre *but no other stake in it than the conduct of his office.* He was not, therefore, to be an actor, a stage-manager or producer, he was not to be a dramatic critic, or a playwright.

My own stage experience made me a supporter of these provisions — it also showed me how much in need our miniature scheme was of a man who could play this part of Director-General. But our work was, of course, not on a scale to induce any being so exceptional, and so little preoccupied, to join us.

It is not possible to say how much we lacked him without making some acknowledgment of what we abundantly had, and in some degree had been blessed with from the dawn of that first of all the Series of Ibsen plays — the Series called into existence by outside initiation, and the first to be financed by funds from an outside group made up of play-goers. One effect of that First Series was to attract to this form of small theatrical enterprise a surprising amount of active support — by active I mean in terms other than money, though money was subscribed too.

Those early backers, Mrs. J. R. Green as convenor and first guarantor; Sir Frederick Pollock and the Hon. Norman Grosvenor as auditors, and presently Mr. Gerald Duckworth as Hon. Secretary, the most generous of all in his gift of time and influence expended on the subscription list.

To these the New Century Theatre had the good fortune to add Mr. Alfred Sutro, playwright of the future and already translator of Maeterlinck and recognized man of letters, who consented to act as our Hon. Manager.

Another acquisition was Mr. H. W. Massingham, described by Mr. Bernard Shaw as 'Editor of the *Chronicle* and Bayreuth pilgrim,' and who was so much more.

The chronicler on the *Pall Mall Gazette* ended his comments by saying that seats for 'John Gabriel Borkman,' 'can be bought at a moderate rate, and Mr. Alfred Sutro will receive the money at Members Mansions, Victoria Street, S.W. The provisional committee consists of Miss Robins, and Messrs. Archer. Massingham and Sutro — a good committee, though we should have liked to see the Norwegian proclivities of Mr. Archer and the severely Hellenic taste of Mr. Massingham tempered by the sober sense of Mr. G. B. Shaw. The auditors, as before, are Mr. Norman Grosvenor and Sir Frederick Pollock, and the treasurer Mr. Gerald Duckworth. And we, as before, wish the enterprise the best of good fortune.'

### HENLEY'S PROLOGUE

Before the Borkman Series ended we had begun preliminary work on the next, presently to find ourselves involved in obstacle after obstacle offered by the part-author of this our first English play, 'Admiral Guinea,' by Robert Louis Stevenson and W. E. Henley.

Letter-writing had to be abandoned for those less ineffectual raids on the tempestuous poet at Barnes. Upon the subject of the cast, Mr. Henley was exigeant beyond any playwright ever heard of — a state of things complicated by the fact, that beyond a manager or two, he didn't know the work of any actor on the English Stage. He knew (or had heard) enough almost to leap out of his bed of suffering and slay me, when I suggested Cissie Loftus for the heroine.

'A Music Hall mime!'

It was true, I said, Miss Loftus had not yet had a chance to distinguish herself in the regular drama. She had great dramatic intelligence as well as great delicacy of style. She was the most natural of all stage people and utterly charming. She would rehearse on approval.

'But there are no *men!*' Like Henry James, Mr. Henley did not believe there were such beings as

191

intelligent actors. He told stories of two out of the more eminent among the Actor-managers, and treated' them to a magnificence of reviling. When I could be heard I said we would not engage either of those gentleman.

In any case, Mr. Henley said, 'The Admiral' had been written in eighteen eighty something. Why hadn't it been played before?

I sat bearing the brunt of a responsibility incurred before I set foot in England. No, no, I was to leave 'Admiral Guinea' alone. They [the dogs in front] 'wouldn't understand this — wouldn't understand that —'

'Write a prologue, then, and *make* them.'

He wrote us a prologue — and Cissie Loftus as Arethusa won all hearts, especially Henley's.

I hasten to add that what I have set down ill represents the sum of interchange with that 'maimed Berserker.' For the truth is, that the railing, enlivening co-operation of Mr. Henley made seeing 'Admiral Guinea' through, a delight.

It was also very hard work; though mercifully less than if I had been playing in the piece myself.


## LXXVII

*34 De Vere Gardens, W.*
Thursday.

Dear Miss Robins.

Will you come to tea HERE on Saturday with the prologue — at 5.30 — or whatever hour suits you?

Or if that isn't convenient to you I will come to *you*. But your presence here would be an honour

and a joy. Then I will at any rate Explain Everything!

Yours very constantly

Henry James

P.S. I *don't* go to Mrs Ward's on Friday.
And I *do* try in the afternoon to hear Mrs Crowe!


PROLOGUE

by William Ernest Henley to

'ADMIRAL GUINEA'

by William Ernest Henley and Robert Louis
Stevenson,

*Spoken by Miss Elizabeth Robins at the Avenue*
*Theatre, Monday, November 29th, 1897.*


Once was an Age, an Age of blood and gold,
An Age of mariners scoundrelly and bold —
Blackbeard and Avory, Singleton, Roberts,—
    Kidd —
An Age which seemed, the while it rolled its
    quid,
Brave with adventure and doubloons and crime,
Rum and the Ebony Trade: when, time on time,
Real Pirates, right Sea-Highwaymen, could mock
The carrion strung at Execution Dock;
And the trim Slaver, with her raking rig,
Her forest of sails, her spars superb and trig.
Held, in a villainous ecstasy of gain,
Her tainted course from Benin to the Main,
And back again for niggers:
When, in fine,
Some thought that Eden blossomed across the
    Line,

193

And some, like Cowper's Newton, lived to tell
That through those latitudes ran the road to
    Hell.

Once was a pair of Friends, who loved to chance
Their feet in any byway of Romance.
They, like two vagabond schoolboys, unafraid
Of stark impossibilities, essayed
To make these Penitent and Impenitent Thieves,
These PEWS and GAUNTS, each man of them with
    his sheaves

Of humour, passion, cruelty, tyranny, life,
Fit shadows for the boards; till in the strife
Of dream with dream, their Slaver-Saint came
    true,
And their Blind Pirate, their resurgent PEW
(A figure of deadly farce in his new birth),
Tap-tapped his way from Orcus back to earth;
And so, their Lover and his Lass made one,
In their best prose this *Admiral* here was done.

One of this Pair sleeps till the crack of doom
Where the great ocean-rollers plunge and boom.
The other waits and wonders what his Friend,
Dead now, and deaf, and silent, were the end
Revealed to his rare spirit, would find to say
If you, his lovers, loved him for this Play.

# LXXVIII

*34 De Vere Gardens, W.*
28th November, 1897.

Dear Miss Robins.

It reconciles me to writing you two words in this form that they acquire so a little more of the distinctness of a friendly Memento.

It is just to say again that it will perhaps be appreciably to the good if you give to 'niggers' not only, so far as possible, the little detached but even the *quoted* sound: as — 'niggers'; * with even a slight pause before it, if the previous part of the phrase, of course, sufficiently consorts with that. Somehow I like even Nell Gwynne mouthing Dryden rather to *quote* 'niggers' than to say it too much off her own bat or too trippingly off her own tongue.

And then do remember to make the pause before your last transition almost long enough to cause some of the audience to wonder if you haven't had a failure of memory: though you can perfectly keep them *really* at ease as to that, really held and waiting, by the direction on them, and control of them, of your face and eye. (You will say it is easy to talk! So it is, before the footlights, for *you!*)

Yours always

Henry James

Things were easier, but not essentially different after the formation of the New Century Thea-

* Line 13 of Prologue.

tre. I had been at this particular sort of work longer than the new Society and I had begun to ask myself more insistently: What did it all come to?

Didn't it come, or wasn't it coming, to be one more of those efforts, however effectual at the moment, doomed to ineffectualness and 'the little day'?

If this was true the reason of it was that we remained in isolation. We didn't 'hitch on' to anything. One looked about and asked what was there to hitch on to?

It had been no part of the little new effort even to try to 'hitch on' to the prevailing actor-manager system. We had come into existence not to oppose that system — a gigantic undertaking that would have argued imbecility as well as inattention to our own business. Our business, as we saw it, was to provide a small side door of escape from the prevailing system and to prove our right to survive by virtue of continuing to be different from what we had turned our back on. But this proved far too innocent a reading of the 'business.' After all that had been done, and approved, what assurance had we, that the venture would survive a year if I took my hand off the wheel? The first condition of effectual survival was that our effort should, by degrees, be worked into the general theatrical life of the time. On what ground could we continue to hope for that? The general theatrical life at the end as at the beginning of the nineties, was shaped and governed by such actors as could secure sufficient financial backing to make them West-End managers. They were not all

geniuses, they were far from being always successful even in their humblest ambitions. But they
could afford failures. It was part of their reason for
existence.

The surface harmony that existed between us
and the managers, not we, but they, were at pains
to deny on application of any real test. We had
cause sometimes to wonder at the heat with which
our venture was derided. Yet this heat was natural.
To a greater degree than I realized at the time,
we had unsettled the more intelligent and ambitious members of the regular companies. We even
had — in other words, Ibsen had — to some extent,
unsettled the public. We unsettled the critics. So
far, then, as the N.C.T. existed at all, for the
Powers in Possession it was privately an irritant
and publicly a reproach.

Mr. James at all events was not disposed to
spare them.

Mrs. Hugh Bell had written to Mr. James for
news of 'Admiral Guinea.'

# LXXIX

*34 De Vere Gardens, W.*
30th November, 1897.

Dear Mrs Hugh.

With all the pleasure in life, if you will excuse
the Remingtonese to which I am now wholly
reduced.

The whole thing was a frank, unmistakeable success. The Prologue went beautifully and was very admirably, artistically and strikingly said; was a real little success in itself, in which the speaker distinctly scored. She said it, really, beautifully, and looked extremely well — with only the fault of staying a little too much at the side of the stage from which she came on — not coming enough to the middle: an error that in a moment of madness I *forgot* to warn her against among two or three things that I wrote to her a day or two before, after she had very kindly given me a hearing of the thing in private. But that was nothing — it didn't interfere at all; and don't mention to her that I mentioned it to you. The only real flaw in the total was the mistake of having the silly little first play — having it, I mean, at all. It wasn't good enough, and elongates a duration (of Bill) which had no need at all of it. However, that is extrinsic, and they drop it, I believe, to-day. The thing itself ['Admiral Guinea'] is most effective; strong, straight, coloured, picturesque, vivid stuff that *all* comes out and all comes home — reaches, carries and arrives, so that even pretty commonish acting can't keep it back or weaken it: it holds up the helpless interpreters with a sort of grip and *makes* them perform. And indeed they are not so bad — and the Pew, with an immense big chance, doing his best, such as it is, all the while. Of course the play is extremely amateurish, and more experience of the horrid business would have made the authors do much more with it. They

198

haven't taken near precautions enough against their great difficulty — that of creating verisimilitude for the freedom with which their old blind scoundrel circulates and manœuvres. And the action has too few wheels — there's a bareness and want of ingenuity in the way it's presented. But what there is of it *does* — and our friend distinctly scores by the way the whole thing (I mean the whole production) is offered and carried through. It can't help, it seems to me, doing her a lot of good — as a fresh illustration of her really fine faculty for — whatever one may call it: stage-managering, presiding over the whole preparation and destiny of the thing and making it as perfect as may be. I confess also to the relief of not having to see her, at that stage of the business, paying with her person before the footlights; affronting, as before, all the further fatigue of the run. I am very glad she goes to you — for all you give her — at the end of the week.

It's a 'commentary,' as the phrase is, that, in the state of the theatre and with the stuff that's produced, none of the idiotic asses of actor-managers should have had the rudimentary intelligence not to let 'Admiral Guinea' languish so long untouched till these comparatively weak and unmonied hands took hold of it. Pew is capable of being composed into an extraordinarily and elaborately picturesque part — and Irving is, in short, well — one knows what!

I have no time, alas, to overflow into more. I hope

you are all well, and I greet the whole house. Do let me know the first time you come to town *not* to hold your court. I wish you a comfortable Christmastide and am yours very constantly

Henry James

## CHAPTER XI

# THE ELLEN TERRY PLAY

After another New Century Theatre production in the spring of 1898, private reasons for
wanting to go to America, chimed in with arrangements to play 'Hedda Gabler' in New York.
Mr. James wrote before I sailed:

## LXXX

*34 De Vere Gardens, W.*
Monday night.

Dear Miss Robins.

I knocked at your door to-day, but with small
hope of finding you — and only left a small sign of
my passage. You must be too furiously busy — too
taken up every moment — and I am much tormented
to think of your having it at all on your mind to
work me into a crevice. *But* I shall be at home all
day to-morrow till 4 — and if you should — by a
miracle — in your gyrations — be within reach of
my bell-pull, it would be a joy to have 20 words with
you. Otherwise — receive my very heartfelt blessing.

My heartiest hopes and prayers go with you. I shan't hear from you; but I shall, so far as possible, haunt those who may have done so. I am much more thrilled than if *I* were going; and shall — after a bit — be much more so still than if I were coming home. I hope you don't voyage wholly alone — but with some friendly face within hail. But you are a mighty spirit and I don't wish you any *banal* wishes. Only come back — if that be not too *banal*. And do everything there. God bless you!

Yours very constantly<br>Henry James

The introduction given me by Mr. James was addressed to that renowned connoisseur, collector, and international hostess, Mrs. John L. Gardner of Boston and other places.

'Mrs. Jack' was the 'Dearest Isabella Gardner' of Mr. James's later letters. Already, in 1898, she was so old a friend of his that he had read to her in 1882 what must have been his first play: a dramatization of 'Daisy Miller.'

## LXXXI

*34 De Vere Gardens, W.*<br>Feb. 10th, 1898.

Dear Miss Robins.

Here is the letter to Mrs Gardner — very brief, as I have already written to her about you, and she knows it is coming. Cultivate her, and let her cultivate *you*.

I figure you to-day as excitedly disembarking —
as it will be your 8th — 9th. All the week I've com-
muned with the elements — and found them here,
at least, auspicious and reassuring. So I hope you
are not reduced to primary paste. Even if you *are*
New York will work you up again. Bring back lots
of it, and of more too. Go to Boston and square the
whole circle.

Yours in all sympathy<br>Henry James

In the next letter he calls me 'Cousin' by reason
of a revelation made to me at this time, probably
at Mrs. J. L. Gardner's, by Mr. George Abbott
James, to whom two of the James letters in the
Lubbock collection are addressed. He is the
'George' James, 'marked for a friend and taken
for a kinsman,' of the glowing pages in *Notes of
a Son and Brother*. He turned out to be the Abbott James whose name was familiar to me from
childhood, though I don't remember meeting him
till 1898. It had never before occurred to me to
connect him with Henry James.

Memory is explicit in recalling from far back
a cousin of my grandmother's, a certain aged but
lively Mrs. Hannah Moorhead James, with bob-
bing pale red ringlets and a step-daughter, who
wasn't very strong, and had to have a companion
to walk out with her! We children knew that
somewhere there was also a favourite stepson,
Abbott. I am not sure that cousin Hannah herself ever knew he was related to Henry James.
None the less she valued Abbott. She would have

liked him to come and see them oftener. But he lived far away and had married a Cabot Lodge.

## LXXXII

*34 De Vere Gardens, W.*
Monday

My dear Cousin!

All hail — all welcome! This is wonderful and delightful. *Do* let me come on Saturday next at 5.15 and stay till 7.15 — 2 good hours, with nobody else. I shall keep this time tight — and arrive sharp. If I don't hear from you adversely. I *yearn* to hear about the strawberry mark — and about everything! Out of what historic scenes you come! The 2 papers about Hedda delighted me. I scarcely contain myself — heaven speed the day! Yours more than ever

Henry James

## LXXXIII

*Lamb House,*
*Rye.*
Oct. 31, 1899

Dear Miss Robins.

I blush to my heels, as Stevenson says, to be writing you to-night a mere hurried note of practical inquiry — breaking my monstrous, graceless silence, at last, to such a graceless end. I hope to do very much better than this very soon — though best of all would be to manage the long-extinguished business of seeing you — if you would generously permit it. Even this I dream of compassing at no very distant day.— *But,* meanwhile, am I mistaken in thinking that you have in your possession a copy of my one-act play that I gave you so long ago to read — the one Ellen Terry has so preposterously treated and which I 'did' into the little published tale? My impression is that I never took it from you again — and that you therefore probably can put your hand on it. If you *can,* and will very kindly post it to me *here* I shall be very, very grateful. I have no other copy, E.T. is in America, and a need has arisen — which I will explain to you later.

There are many, many things I want to say to you and to ask of you; but it is long past midnight, and I am very tired, and my eyes and my hand ache. It is, however, a deep satisfaction to me — please believe it — to find myself even in this so partial, so incomplete communication with you. I shall dig it deeper as soon as I can grasp the silver spade. I hear of you sometimes even here and in good terms that are a joy to yours, dear Miss Robins, very contritely and constantly

Henry James

## LXXXIV

*34 De Vere Gardens, W.*
Wednesday.

Dear Miss Robins.

I have been so taxingly busy that I haven't had
— or found — the manners to answer your so genial
note about the small play — and now I am *not* answering it because on the stroke of three I have to
go down to Rye for 2 days and then return only to
go elsewhere again till Monday. All this time I shall
be much taken up — so I sadly fear I can't now say
two or three things I much want. I didn't, I fear,
make clear to you that the play isn't — literally —
free — I mean the connection with E.T. formally
broken. She will never produce it — but we rub on
together a bit longer. Alas, I've made a *tale* of ifs —
and the Tale's to be published. Three things — the
latter in particular didn't I mention to you? But we
must *talk* of them — *well*: next week. Any p.m. you
name. Name *any* and forgive the rude haste — and
foul blots — of yours always

Henry James

P.S. My re-writing of the dialogue has *so* bettered it!

I wrote on the margin of the next letter: 'I
wished luck to the Ellen Terry play.'

## LXXXV

*34 De Vere Gardens, W.*, Tuesday.
Dear Miss Robins.

In half an hour more your kind note would have crossed with this — for this is what I was on the very edge, this a.m. of writing to you. I wanted to give you my blessing on your — on our — inevitable year; and I wanted to have a chance moreover to give it in person. So my note was to have been, as I didn't know you were out of town, an appeal for an hour at which I might find you at home. Let me thank you, however, first for your benevolent hopes and expressions — they flutter about the dark void like white-winged doves or 'airs from heaven.' (I call it a dark void not tragically,— but wearily). Then let me appeal, as I meant to, for an hour. Won't you let me know of one — even *after* dinner would work in very well — as soon as you come back? I am very unengaged, thank God, just now, having foresworn all manner of dining out (I dine to-night at Lady Lewis's!) and being therefore in possession of lots of evenings. We might arrange then to do a play, though all the plays are nought. When *do* you come home? I must, whenever that is, try to bless those who keep you. Please give my love to them — especially to Mrs Florence and Mr Hugh, and Master Hugo.

Yours, dear Miss Robins, right constantly

Henry James

## LXXXVI

*Lamb House,*
*Rye,*
Nov. 5th, 1899

Dear Miss Robins.

I have meant these two or three days to thank you kindly for sending me the copy of the little Play — with which I am happy to say Ellen Terry's preposterous connection has definitely ceased, and about which I shouldn't have troubled you (in this particular manner) were it not for circumstances over which I have no control — as it were. Some months ago I received 2 pressing requests for the play (requests founded on the perusal of the Tale;) each of which I said a definite Nay to — one from G. Alexander, one from F. Robertson. But since then a strong motive, sordidly pecuniary (the result of Want of Money) has arisen and if the thing (that is, disposing of it) can bring me a sum that I have attached to it as a price, I can't afford *not* so to dispose of it — little heart as I have. I have no choice. But it may be that this idea won't be realized — I don't know yet; and in that case things will be as they were before (save that Miss T. will be out of it,) and I will send you back the affair with the greatest pleasure — subject to our talking of it on the first opportunity. If my possible arrangement *does* take place I will do you a much *better* one act; for I distinctly *can*. Please excuse, again, this con-

208

tracted and condensed communication: I have, for the moment, my hands very full. I am working toward an interval in my too long exile from London, and then — when the interval comes — I propose, with your permission, to haunt your steep staircase and dog your swift step. I desire more news of you than I dare to imagine you will easily give me — so easily, that is, as by my asking for it thus. The news I occasionally catch is good — isn't it? But you won't even tell me that. No matter — it has that air,— and at any rate I very heartily desire so to read it. Believe me

Yours very particularly

Henry James

## LXXXVII

*Lamb House,*
*Rye.*

Dear Miss Robins.

I send you back poor Mrs Gracedew, (even as she has been returned on *my* hands, after all:) for you to have and to hold, to do what you like with — above all to *produce,* absolutely at your freedom and discretion, when the right occasion rises! Obviously, in the light of the 'story,' in the vol. of the '2 Magics', there is much more to be got out of her and put into her; and indeed that tale constitutes for her rather a unique and rich prompt-book. The *real* difficulty in the whole thing is *compression* — to play

209

in an hour; for the action is already so close and tightly logical. Ellen T. wanted 'half an hour taken out' of her — and appeared to look to me to do that without further guarantee or support, in a spirit of sublime and ideal devotion. Alexander 4 or 5 months ago wrote me urgently: 'Won't you let me have the play for me and Miss Fay Davis?' And when I — after the interval — read it to him — sounding him first: 'Will you *now* have it? — the enclosed is his urbane and inspiring reply. Are you surprised that I'm infatuated with the theatre? *Destroy*, please, the urbane and inspiring one. It will heal my wounds — *some* on 'em — to talk, as soon as occasion offers — with you. The play goes back to-morrow; this alone to-night.

Yours, in haste, always<br>Henry James

Sunday p.m.

LXXXVIII

34 De Vere Gardens, W.<br>Wednesday

Dear Miss Robins.

Forgive my long delay — there have been reasons. But here *is* the one-act fairy-tale. I can *re-write* it much better. I will explain when I see you what I mean.

Yours ever<br>Henry James

The New Century Theatre had made known its hope to produce 'Peer Gynt' with the Grieg music.

Apart from difficulties of the moment in securing the right people for this tremendous undertaking, the Committee felt the need of discouraging the reproach that we were always falling back on Ibsen. So far only one of our Series — the latest — had represented the work of the younger generation. This bill was made up of a one-act play by Margaret Young and 'Grierson's Way' in four acts by H. V. Esmond, who was considered by many to be the most promising of the coming men. These performances left us with ample funds for another Series.

I can vouch for the fact that up to the end of 1899 (when a call came that was to take me too far away for any following of theatre affairs) there was no slackening on the part of the N.C.T. Committee in the keen look out for work of sound quality. We seemed to be always reading plays. Anything promising was passed on first to Mr. Archer. His report on Mr. James's Ellen Terry play, a report designed to be shown, if I thought best, covers nearly three pages of closely written type. It begins: 'I think the enclosed a gem with a single flaw,' and winds up 'On the whole I think the piece a delightful one, which a few quite inessential alterations ought to render (with good acting) genuinely successful and popular.'

I do not remember, now, the precise steps by which the N.C.T. came to the decision not to do 'Mrs. Gracedew.' I am sure the decision did not greatly disappoint or even surprise the author, but I think it marked a period.

While Mr. James retained, with any force or continuity, the idea of his own practical connection with the theatre, he and I had his hopes as well as mine, for a common bond. As long as he could believe, and I could hope, that I might venture again to play one of his graceful and gracious ladies, or make myself responsible for production of one of his plays, he would naturally feel there was still a possibility of making something, to the general gain, out of me as 'colleague.' The time never came. This was not only because of my doubt in my own success, but very much because of anxiety as to what my failure (whether as actress or producer) would mean, after all he had gone through, to Henry James. I do not remember our formulating the view, but I think we realized that the time had come when, as a passionate personal interest, the Theatre chapter had closed. That is to say the stage door had closed; for I need hardly count the two later occasions, when under pressure from others, the stage door opened for me. Nor in Mr. James's case need I count the production eight or nine years later of 'The High Bid' on tour,* since to do so is to recall the fact that the hoped-for result, appearance in a regular night bill for a London run, was never realized.

The stage door closed for both Mr. James and me, with no slam from either of us. It closed quietly, gently, without bitterness, without even the decency of sharp regret.

We had not expected it would be so with me. When people remonstrated at my failing to re-

* This was Ellen Terry's 'Mrs. Gracedew' expanded to 3 acts and produced by Johnstone Forbes-Robertson.

spond to this opportunity or that, when they prophesied repentance 'after it is too late,' I wasn't at all sure there might not be something in it. Very likely I *would* sit at home in the silence, and 'at 8 p.m.' lift miserable eyes to the clock, as they promised, and say: 'Now the curtain is going up. Somebody else is playing the great part —

Yes, I could not hope to escape that.

The odd thing is, I did escape. I never remembered to notice it was curtain-raising time. I never indulged the appropriate sentiment. There was always something else happening.

Few of these happenings were calculated to enlist Mr. James's sympathy. Yet that is just what never failed me. And in this I find the reason for my valuing, perhaps, most of all, those kindnesses of his that marked the years after our common Theatre-love grew cold.

## CHAPTER XII

# AFTER THE STAGE DOOR CLOSED

In the Introduction a word was said about Participation. It is of course the essence of all friendship. The difference lies in the degree of the Participation and the diversity of ground covered.

As I go on, I come to feel that by arranging in little groups, a selection of these later letters that most particularly illustrate the genius for Participation, I can come nearest to paying my belated tribute to a delicate, various element in Mr. James's friendship.

The half-dozen notes and letters that follow, being mostly without sufficient internal evidence, I am not able to say whether the 'tales' Mr. James wanted to hear, had to do with Scotland, or with the hermit life he professed to be curious about at the Edward Greys' Hampshire Fishing Cottage; or happenings in the Black Forest, Switzerland, Paris, Bayreuth or again and again, Florida. I only know he was good to take things home to.

As Mr. Percy Lubbock says in one of those prefaces indispensable to the patient follower of the course of Mr. James's life '... he liked to enter into other people's thought and to meet them on their own ground. There his natural kindliness and his keen dramatic interest were both satisfied at once.'

To that very true observation, this seems to be the place to add a further explanation of the reason Mr. James wanted to hear about my doings and continued, among other activities, to 'come and read.'

First, a word about the reading. For long, I did not know that I was not the good audience he deserved and that I fondly dreamed I was. For I took pains. I had seen his look of anguish when in the middle of a page someone would interrupt. I had heard his description — never to be forgotten — of reading to a lady who had allowed tea, positively encouraged, *tea!* to be violently introduced into the scene, and relentlessly spread in his presence!

I was careful to make tea, myself, at the judicious moment. Any air of haste or skimped time during the reading I knew to be abhorrent. My happy invention, as I fatuously believed, to create an atmosphere of utter, listening quiet — met little success. Mrs. W. K. Clifford reported, for our common good, that there were occasions when Henry James found me inexpressive '. . . She doesn't . . . er . . . doesn't *say* . . .' The sobering thought comes, perhaps she didn't even 'look' — for I (no needlewoman except in the special exigency) would bend over a piece of work; interminable and therefore advertising the Unhurried State; mechanical, and therefore leaving full attention free, tranquil, absorbed in the sounding voice and the play of mind.

If I did not speak for myself *then*, I hope I have

successfully resisted the temptation to speak, now, for Mr. James. He speaks for himself, here. My part (hampered in this section for the reasons of inadequate dating, etc., given above) has been to do anything I can to make the letters — and thereby the circumstances they touch — a little clearer; that is, to restore to the letters some of the clearness, some of the significance which was theirs when they were written. Mr. James's literary or other opinions, however clearly spoken by himself, I make no pretence to report — though, I have said that, as time went on, he talked more and more about books, and that, in those days, his condemnation spared few. I speak of the days immediately under review. Mr. James had not yet come into that region of later friendships, begun on literary grounds, tending on one side towards discipleship, and on the other culminating in *Notes on Novelists*. I have meant to show the effect his earlier, magnificently uncompromising, attitude had on one of his friends, because this effect in its turn reacted on himself. He wrote truly of the Henry James of that period: 'I *am* damned critical — for it's the only thing to be, and all else is damned humbug.'

I won't deny the sheer excitement of looking on at the smashing of those reputations I thought too cheaply won. But naturally, the spectacle bred a wholesome discretion. It bred, too, something like supersensitiveness to the effect on *him* of the unleashing of that terrific power to deride, to wither, to reduce to nothingness.

There was no need to tell me, as he later told another and more intimate correspondent, that he 'could not bear tragedy.' For one thing, I knew it wasn't true, and, for another, his bearing it cost him too much. What I found myself unconsciously playing for was the glint of amusement that would cross the tragic face. Dearly I loved making him produce those signs that did duty for laughter, and I am sure that the reason he came to hear my 'adventures' was because those I presented him were, as a rule, selected with care. I never lost sight of that enemy of his, the melancholy that only his deepest joy could master. Fortunately for him and for us all, the deepest joy — an unshakable belief in his genius — never failed him. Whatever other reward was lacking, he found *his* in the religious exercise of his craft, his Faith. I hear his sombre voice, I see the ironic pride on that mask of melancholy, as he would say of a piece of work he had just finished — crowning it as if with the authentic bay — 'it is of an *ingenuity*!

Among notes, letters, and telegrams not included here, there are many similar to those on the next few pages. In sum, they add to the fragment of Mr. James's life represented by this book, not only the small fact that he had the impulse to 'come and read,' or hear stories *viva voce* — but that the impulse visited him so often and over so long a time.

## LXXXIX

*34 De Vere Gardens, W.*
Thursday.

Dear Miss Robins.

Let us call it, on Monday evening, *8.30* if that suits you; for we must have a good margin of time. I shall have tea and buns before I leave home (buns are filling — *staying,*) and then perhaps between Acts 2nd and 3rd you will give me what we call in the bright home of the setting sun, a 'bite.' A very, very restricted one will amply suffice — even another mere bun (if there *be* such a thing as a 'mere' bun) would do. Yes, I have said Yea to Miss Kingsley — and I trust that on both occasions the Frock will be much to the fore. *Do* listen in the Frock — though it makes me ask myself what then I shall *read* in: to keep it proper company.

I want to ask you about Miss —— [an excellent old actress fallen on evil days] — who has just — this a.m. — written so *desperate* a letter. Can one do *anything* for her? — Carr as yet only writes me asking for a delay of judgment on my piece — till he has produced his Xmas child's comedy. It makes me fear he *may* say Yea to it — which I now don't particularly want.

Yours always
Henry James

## XC

*34 De Vere Gardens, W.*
October 31st

Dear Miss Robins.

I didn't know you were back; and I revel in the circumstances! I fly to your door this afternoon — but shall have to come early — in order to be at a bothersome appointment at 6. If the appointment fails, as it may, I shall try and recover you at 6.15 — or 30. This is a bad week with me and I don't know just yet what other day and hour to propose; but shall speedily take thought. Next week will be better. I am hungry indeed for your traveller's tales — and all agape in advance. I hope you return with wonderfully girded loins — as it were! Will you kindly say to Mrs Bell whose very petit mot I received, that I am watching the moment to get to her even as a cat a mouse!

Yours always
Henry James

## XCI

*34 De Vere Gardens, W.*

Dear Miss Robins.

I don't know if you are back in town again; but I yearn to do so. The best way to let me will be surely to say some evening next week on which we may have that too-deferred 'swarry' . . . .

219

Won't you name your own evening to dine with me and go to something — *not* **P.** the **G.** ['Peter the Great']? *I* should like our national Circus — at Olympia — as near and handy! — unless you *propose* something. But *do*, please, propose your company, — for 17th, 18th, 19th or *any* evening? It's ages — more than ever before. I hope you have brought back muscle and sinew from Red Barns.

Yours, dear Miss Robins, always

Henry James

Wednesday


## XCII

*34 De Vere Gardens, W.*
Wednesday

Dear Miss Robins.

All thanks for your news. I am unspeakably thrilled and will come in to-morrow Thursday at 4.30.

Yours ever

Henry James


## XCIII

*34 De Vere Gardens, W.*
October 13th, 1896

Dear Miss Robins.

I heard yesterday that you are in town — after being (since my own recent return and day to day continuance) under the lively, or rather deadly, delusion that you are *not*. This adds fuel to the flame of my desire to see you. May I not do so ( come to you for that delightful purpose) at some time that you yourself will kindly fix?

Have you not, in these more spacious times, *an evening* free? — Thursday, Friday, Saturday, Sunday? I mean after dinner — toward 9? I will thump at your door on any one of these that you are so good as to mention — bringing a list of inquiries and eagernesses as long as my arm — of greetings and good wishes as long as my leg! Yours, dear Miss Robins, very constantly

Henry James

## XCIV

*105 Pall Mall, S.W.*

Dear Elizabeth Robins.

How kind you are and what a luxury again — and a small recapture of other days — to be treating with you on the dear old London basis!

On Tuesday night without fail, then, at 9 o'clock.

Yours ever
Henry James

Sunday a.m.

## XCV

Dear Miss Robins.

Just a word to express (without the smallest call
for a rejoinder on your part,) my grateful sense of
the humanity of your little letter — with its implica-
tion — so kind — of your perception that I am *not,*
and have not been, given over, at this distance, to
mere unsociable cold-shoulderism and general shut-
ters-up insensibility, as some of my old friends have
appeared to infer. I've had good reasons, the best,
for much exile from town, and much concentration
and abstraction and even taciturnity; but I can assure you that I am still warm and sentient beneath
these mufflings, and particularly accessible to whatever concerns *you.* Therefore your few words on that
theme have a great value to me. The long continuity
of time I have put in here will have a break after
the New Year, and my idea is *then* (when I do come
up,) to be in town till May. I still possess, thank
heaven, De Vere Gardens (or an infinitesimal fraction of it,) though I have lent my flat for a longish
time to my brother and his wife; he being rather
gravely ill there; and that constitutes at all events
a solid link. But how I shall enjoy putting myself
in your hands, and if you'll allow me, — being

222

purged of all arrears and made modern, recent, actual. I daresay I shall be in the field when you come back from Yorkshire and then I shall ask you to 'take' me everywhere. I shall be able to do little alone.

Yours very constantly

Henry James

With the subject of the oddest of my traveller's tales Mr. James himself had, almost incredibly, a personal association.

One of the 'life-chances' too far-fetched to be used in fiction was that Arctic gold, in the concrete form of the Klondyke, entered as intimately and lastingly into Mr. James's existence as into mine. Differences in the conception of what constitutes 'fortune' can seldom have been presented by a contrast more fantastic than that Henry James's idea of a 'find' ('of striking it rich') was Lamb house, Rye, and that he only *just* didn't miss it by the narrow margin of a preference on the part of the English owner of the house for joining in the Klondyke Rush of 1897. By the end of '99 I was finding intolerable the lack of direct news from those regions and the assumption on the part of the authorities of the death, there, of my youngest brother. The natural enough plan of my going to investigate, saw Mr. James pass from incredulity to horror and by faithful degrees back to serviceable kindness.

To explain the next letter it must be recalled that, towards the end of the New Century Theatre time, I had written an historical melodrama in collaboration with a friend on the subject of

223

Benvenuto Cellini. We had come to feel the play needed further work — which, neither my collaborator nor I had time to give. With the collaborator's consent I invoked Mr. James, whose hand had helped 'Mariana' in her need. But when it was made clear that I was bent upon being on the other side of the world (ready to sail from my Pacific port the moment the ice had broken in the Behring Sea) Mr. Beerbohm Tree, who had the play under consideration, made up his mind to accept 'Benvenuto' without revision. He signed a contract with a penalty-clause for non-production within a given time. This agreement and a copy of the play, were left in Mr. James's keeping.

## XCVI

*The Athenæum,*
*Pall Mall, S.W.*
March 20th 1900

Dear Miss Robins.

I can easily understand how squeezed and pressed you must be, with all you have to do and think of — how more than hustled and hurried; — and our tackling of Benvenuto would indeed be a big job. Therefore I acquiesce — with a pang! But I had rather sink the play than that you should take a precaution the less. Take them *all*, without exception, and may they see you safely and happily through and bring you richly and gloriously back. Then we will make up our loss — and I shall perhaps not be wholly of disservice in bringing you gently down again to our smaller æsthetic perspective. But don't think of that meanwhile: go truly forth into the immensity, and trust *me*, in particular, to keep in my pocket for you, the key of the little elegant cabinet. I will hold it safe and the lock will play again at my touch. May almighty powers keep step with you!

Yours, please believe me, always and ever

Henry James

## CHAPTER XIII

# 'BEDSIDE MANNER'

My last word from the far North before I left England had told of a great mortality from typhoid raging among the miners.

After forty-four days in the new gold camp on the coast of the Behring Sea, my brother and I had parted with no suspicion that each was infected by the fever. We had planned to meet in San Francisco or Kentucky after we had discharged our obligations — his being certain services undertaken at Cape Nome; mine, to cover the 1700 miles of waterway between St. Michael's and the Klondyke and there to complete the commission I had undertaken for a London editor.

The 'good lady' of Mr. James's letter to Mrs. Hugh Bell was the friend of my early youth (then visiting London) Mrs. Erskine Clement Waters of Boston. This letter was written after my third relapse while I was nearing the end of nine weeks at a hospital in the Pacific Coast seaport — my place of landing on the way 'home.'

*Lamb House,*
*Rye.*
September 27th 1900.

Dear Mrs Bell.

Most kind and interesting — more than that, most heroic — your tour de force of a railway letter, which adds to the obligation your telegram of 2 days since placed me under. *I* write railway letters in my chair; *my* hand bounces without the aid of 50 miles an hour; and my performances, in short, are but tours de faiblesse. You tell me things I've all along not known; for I've sat in the deepest darkness. Cramponnons-nous to the good doctor's good words — even though they *be* not overwhelmingly sustaining. They do, I agree with you, fall a little short; but every day pieces them a little along; and after all one can't say better than that a person who has been so perilously ill is still successfully resisting after it. One must believe in this lady's strength when one has known it, seen it, so tried. Yes, yes — we shall see it tried again. It won't be for this time. She is panoramic — and NOT au bout de son rouleau. The best is to come. But I *have* been out of it all. It's the 1st I know of the successful rapprochement to the other brother — awfully interesting as it is, — but again, I agree, in its actual feature, terrific. *He* must get well for *her* to. Doubtless, doubtless, news coming to her of *his* disaster (I mean collapse — if she even knows he *is* ill; but it must have been kept from her!) would have the gravest result. And heaven knows what care *he* has! But it's a *case* — and she rules her cases. The star that saves her will do so by saving *him*. We must believe it from day-to-day. Meanwhile I don't envy you the opening of your telegrams. Let us pay, in short, for a 100,000 Masses. I feel as depleted, from mere interest, as if I *had* paid. And I've had from Heinemann the manifesto — brave manifesto — from the good lady qui nous tombe des nuées. Who *is* the good lady? There is so much more for you to tell me. I wish I wasn't so far, so busy, so utterly tied: I would dash up to your wild Northern shore — wild enough surely as I write; for our tame Southern is to-day in convulsions. I would ask you many more things, and I would assist at your midnight mass. I can't even get at the good lady. Excuse my incoherence. I didn't in the least know of your husband's illness, admirable man. I shouldn't have been silent about it had I dreamed. How sorry a summer, and how combined an anxiety. I gather he is more than convalescent, and I grasp his hand in tender friendship. Please assure him of my deep participation. The history of Tree and the Play &c. — this is another matter darkly sealed to my sense. I supposed the play non-produced by her absence only — waiting for her, needing her return. But if there has been base treachery par dessus le marché, there has been only what — in these relations — there *had* to be, and in hogsheads. What miseries, all round! I fix my thoughts on Anne Ritchie and her beautiful identity, installed at your fireside to uplift and console a bit my sad vision. Say to her, please, that my sore soul rests on her. I am staring at her hard — to clear the picture, to cool my eyes. But they stray ever so kindly over the rest of your house, and attach themselves, after all, finally to its leading lady — with all the intensity with which I am, dear Mrs Bell, yours very constantly

Henry James


'The Bentinck Street limbo' of the next letter was Mr. James's name for the London nursing home where I was till I moved on from place to place in a search for health that lasted nearly two years.

Almost any story of human relationship that has not ended in violence, or the chill of alienation, comes to a place where it touches illness, or that more searching trial of friendship, protracted convalescence. The young may easily be forgiven for not wanting to hear this chapter — for frankly skipping it. It doesn't come into their rôle — as yet.

But older people are not without some interest in a stage of the Journey that most of them have taken. They recognize the landmarks. They, too, have been in the Blind Alley; they have stood later at the Aussichtspünkte and have admitted that these aspects are not without claim to being Sehenswürdigkeiten. Whether, as Sir Thomas

229

Browne says, there is a Sapor in all ailments — there is in illness a power, to tell us something about our friends, denied to the eloquence of health.

Mr. James had his own incomparable way of adapting his literary manner to the bedside and the bath chair. Sympathy with another's predicament (especially with mine, coming as it did after such expenditure on his part of remonstrance and warning) might, without his being able to prevent it, have taken on an air of: 'Didn't I tell you so?' Or, from a man whose view of life was as melancholy as Henry James's, sympathy might, one would think, take the lugubrious form of: 'What else is to be expected in such a world?' That this was far from being the form, was due not only to the fact that the man of genius is not the one to convince us life isn't worth living — his power to feel, and to express, are seen too clearly as a glorious vindication of that value he may deny. Moreover, the Henry James brand of sympathy was a blessing to his friends because, touched as it unfailingly was with ironic humour, it was as tonic in our days of feebleness, as it had sometimes been mere impediment in the days of insolent health. Certainly his gift for participation here seems in its effect to have prompted pages as like him, and as little like others, as anything of his writing.

In these notes to the bed-bound or the convalescent, nothing (after their undertone of concern) was so reviving as his trick of humorous exaggeration. At your lowest, he could make you smile, sometimes teach you again to laugh outright at his involutions and hyperboles dashed with news of the world outside. He would throw

in a word about the fresh field of adventure opening to my friend Sir George Robertson 'the hero
of Chitral,' and tell about dear Lucy Clifford's
'current adventure' and Archer's article on it. He
would hearten the invalid with a healing sympathy and say next whom he sat at dinner in the
house of a common friend; how, afterward, Mrs.
Beerbohm Tree had enlivened the occasion with
an imitation 'which she does wondrously' of Mrs.
Patrick Campbell; how Mr. Tree's 'Twelfth
Night' (Oh, the echoes!) has a prospect of a run,
how Mrs. Hugh Bell having set off for a visit to
her brother-in-law, Sir Frank Lascelles, at the
British Embassy in Berlin (she, with her two
young daughters, in readiness to make their curt-
sies at the Imperial Schleppencour) found on
arrival the whole gay prospect blacked out by the
Kaiser's plunging the German court into deepest
mourning on hearing of the death of Queen Victoria — all *that,* without loss of a syllable or an
accent, conveyed to the prepared mind, in a single
phrase: 'her dressy pilgrimage all blighted.' He
had already told how, in England, what he called
'the public picture' had cast all others into the
shade; how with our friend Mrs. J. R. Green he
had walked home from the historic funeral — impressed, yet not able to resist the temptation of
conveying the universality of participation by
saying 'London, London-like made a sort of "large-
and-early" of the Queen's funeral.'

My dear Elizabeth Robins.

I have too miserably delayed to act upon the immediate impulse to write to you that I became conscious of as soon as I heard, at the beginning of the week, that you had sought precious protection from a too importunate world. And the reason of my delay has been, truly, that no such protection has spread its mantle over *me*. I had several over-crowded days away from this place and then I came back here to arrears and a guest. The guest and the arrears, between them, have given me much to do, and I have snatched this tardy hour by setting the former down to his own share of the latter at a letter-writing table in the drawingroom. Also, through all this, I have felt myself in harmony with the admirable, the not-sufficiently-to-be-praised idea of your being let alone. It was a great sorrow not to be able to see you on Monday, but I would gladly pay for your right regimen by a dozen personal pains. I in fact fairly revel in your retirement and jubilate over your surrender. You got well too fast and we are only putting in the slowness, like so many dropped stitches of the silver thread, *now*. The reckoning will soon be complete and then our conscience, the general one, and your condition, will

all be good together. I daresay we shall both re-
emerge on the tense old town at about the same
moment, as I come up there soon after Xmas for
as long a stay as possible. I think I got the sidewind
there, the other day, of some of the breezes set
a-blowing so straight down your throat, and there
would have been matters for discourse among them
all could I only have seen you. But luckily these
things are such as will gain by keeping. Dear Lucy
Clifford, for instance, led me through the dark
labyrinth of her current adventure — and I've just
read her play over again in the light of the labyrinth
and of Archer's article on it (not having been able
to see it given.) What above all comes home to me
is the error of not grappling with the black Demon
(i.e. the dire scenic form) till your store of wiles for
trapping him is equal to *his* wondrous assortment
of the same for tripping you up, and serious and discreet as is, for instance, the play in question, it seems
to me to put it to one forcibly that that general subject has absolutely nothing more to give on the
merely — on the *at all* — sentimental side. That has
been too utterly discounted. A wholly different kind
of interest, only I judge, can be wrenched from
it — the ironic, the satiric, the scientific, or whatever, till the sentimental, withdrawal into some
*Bentinck St.* limbo, can bloom again. But I mustn't
pretend to sound these depths at this hour and to
your detached mind. It's past midnight — I see a
British nurse glare with deprecation at your occu-

pied face. Therefore become blank and vague — become British too — let everything go that it may come back a hundredfold. I hope you are living into resignation — or, better still, into some good gross greedy materialism. That is the real refuge. Only give me a little time and I will write again. I send this to kind Mrs Waters — having no number for you. Schlafen Sie recht wouhl and believe me very watchfully and waitingly yours

Henry James

## XCIX

The Reform Club<br>Feb. 9th 1901

Dear Elizabeth Robins.

... I have been acutely conscious of your having sought, in your retreat, an unmolested peace — and possibly of your being forbidden the mingled cup that the postman so cynically holds to us. ...

You've been on the whole pretty well out of these late sombre, though rather picturesque events — with London a thing of squashing crowds and over-done talk and vain repetition, to myself, and after long absence, there is a certain charm in the renewal — the exaggeration — of the once-familiar muchness and quantity; but I represent to myself that you have been constantly, till now, so up to your chin in the high tides of the world, that, you lie with conscious relief, and with envy quite stilled, on the quiet

Yours, dear Miss Robins most truly
Henry James.

golden sands. This is a clumsy manner of saying that I don't believe you would have left Paignton if you could. I'm extremely sorry your time there coincides — with such uncanny neatness — with my time here; but I recall that I too found it peaceful and placid when, at a period, I used to walk over there — and well beyond — from Torquay. I hope you can read, and I am sure you can write; and if you can't manage arithmetic, so much the better. I wish I had a cornucopia of luscious news to empty into your lap. But the public picture has somehow cast all others into the shade. London made, London-like, a sort of 'large — and early' of the Queen's funeral — which was impressive and really picturesque. . . . And there are spectacles and suspenses and changes for the future — some of which you must come up in time for. We somehow feel that the new regime will have features — and wish it would only, or above all, soon have that of ending the [Boer] War. It will be full of interesting personal and social questions. However, you will find these more mature later on.

I see many of your friends, and I find they believe you to be consolidating your genius and renewing your youth — which is a conviction, a fundamental doctrine, that draws us closer together. I dined with the G. Lewises on Thursday — and sat next Mrs B ——, whom I found myself quite loving . . . The rest had their eternal youth — with the exception of ——, who had her eternal old age. I walked home from the Queen's funeral with Mrs Green, whom

I find troubled about many things — too troubled perhaps, and about too many. But on some of them I much feel with her. The Bells have ceased to chime — here — and you knew, of course, of her dressy Berlin pilgrimage all blighted on her arrival. Hugh B. didn't, when I last saw him here, seem to have as much of the good of being 'better' as one could wish, but I daresay it has grown on him since. I haven't been to the sign of a play — my nearest approach was seeing Mrs B. Tree, the other night, imitate (at the Lewis's,) Mrs P. Campbell (which she does wondrously. She could *perfectly* do her parts.) I believe Tree's *12th Night* has the prospect of a run, and the St. James's 'Haddon Chambers' possibly not. Forgive so meagre a budget, and don't *dream* of acknowledging it. I hope you get a good deal of lying on your sofa and looking at Torbay. I hope the latter is often blue and that the sense of Devonshire 'sort of' wraps you about. I inconsistenly, also, hope — grossly and egotistically tumble into it — that you are likely to come back before I return to the country; but even if you don't I shall still be unfailingly yours

Henry James

# C

Dear Elizabeth Robins.

How generous and beneficent your beautiful return for my weak and belated little letter! It gives me real joy, and I enter unreservedly into both the causes and the effects of your prolonged absence from this vast and intimate city. It's too intimate for its size, and, already again, if *I* didn't have my NURSING HOME in the background, as a retreat and a remedy, I should, I fear, find it necessary to have one final and fatal good quarrel with the Purgatory-Paradise. Paradise Paignton with a grenadier Angel at the Gate sounds to me truly ideal for you, and as the sight of anything well done and highly finished is always delightful to me, I can't tell you how I rejoice to see you really elaborating your convalescence. I am convinced that of all your creations it will be the one to bring you most glory and most guineas. I can see that my addressing you at One of the N. H.'s, [Nursing Homes] must indeed have struck you as inadequate, but I was markedly anxious my letter shouldn't be delayed, and 'Soquel' *is* a very difficult name to remember. One broods over its origin and even its pronunciation. But I cherish its prospectus, and if ever I have any time to get better, (get good enough, that is, to make it worth while,) I shall enter into relations with your archangel of the flaming sword — I quite adore her already. And I adore the idea that you are as a friend of mine always calls it, prosperously cerebrating. Here, just now, we write it only with an *l* — and we seem to do it, in that form, all the time. I take the greatest interest in the advent of your Brother, though I don't focus him at all, and I congratulate you heartily on the sight of the concussion — in his life and conversation — of the wild and the tame West. Don't tame *him* too much before we have the pleasure of seeing him here. I am much wondering if there is any service I can render him? — as I should be so glad to do if he wishes to come up to London for a few days. But probably the Grenadier has him quite in her knapsack. I'm sorry to gather I was wrong about Mrs B ——! I wasn't mad over her, but à quoi se fier? I saw Mrs Clifford last night and she was extremely playful. She has, in this direction, great spirit, but an inadequate sense of difficulty and danger. However, it serves her well, for she tells me that she has clear testimony that her Kendal play, though hated by Mrs K., is never given but to the fullest houses. But why do I talk to you of Kendalisms? . . .

Believe me yours ever so faithfully

Henry James

P.S. I've just been talking with Sir George Robertson, who now wants to go to China.

*Lamb House,*
*Rye.*
April 22nd, 1901

My Dear Elizabeth Robins.

... Don't answer me, don't even — if still forbidden you — *think* of me: only be breathed upon by my own anxious and well-meaning thought — in as benedictory a manner as possible. That thought, all this weary winter, has been constantly with you, counting the days of your long eclipse and trying to read into it all sorts of consoling senses. Now that I am down here, with rather anxiety-breeding relatives in my house (I mean my brother, ill — though better — and his wife and daughter,) I seem to feel rather more than less built out, by adverse things, from converse with you: yet all the while cherishing the idea that the end of the tunnel is really nearer and attracting my eyes to the daylight that I refuse to believe you yourself don't see. May it brighten and broaden from this hour. This is only a vague, sketchy, affectionate sign in the still-prevailing dimness. I haven't much to tell you save that we don't grow one least little scrap used to missing you, and that, after 3 or 4 winter months of London, I am committed again to this theory of solitude and practice of company. Yet even so there is no one near me with whom I can especially talk of you! Please see much of that in this confused and impatient demonstration. . . .

We are having here at last lovely days, and I hope they beneficently shine upon you. Believe me always devotedly yours

Henry James

If I had not later in convalescence been still too much of an invalid, for a time, to share with my beloved hostess, her glorious long hours in the galleries of Florence, I should never have known that city was the place in all the world that Henry James loved best. Following his instructions, I saw of it what I could from a carriage, and with such an opener-of-doors as Caroline Grosvenor, I ran no risk of forgetting his charge: 'go to all the old villas you can get into.' So it was that no time was lost in visiting Nuti, lunching at the Villa Medici, and making real acquaintance with Chiochini. For, this last I was to know best of all (except Il Palmerino *) sitting long hours in her garden with that fine flower of the English tradition Lady Airlie of the stately mien and the wool-white hair, hair curled into a formality that vied with the head-dress of an Egyptian Queen. Good sound talk the Chiochini hostess dealt in, diversified once, as I remember, by an exchange of pungent comment with her brother Monsignor Stanley. Clearly, they enjoyed cutting and thrusting at each other. As he paced the terrace after dinner — a little out of easy range, I thought, of

* Not one of the 'old villas' specially prescribed, but the home made for herself by the brilliant woman of letters, Vernon Lee — congenial meeting place for writers, artists and worldlings.

our two chairs — he delivered himself on a lifted note, that charged his sister, with incorrigible misuse of Italian idiom. His own accuracy was instantly challenged, for only I seemed to be impressed either by his learning or his swinging cassock of ravishing violet silk. '*You*, certainly, ought to know Italian better after so many years!' said Lady Airlie, though her brother knew quite enough to be made Bishop of Emmaus.

One of the curiosities of memory is that it may be kept clearer by a single phrase, by a light phrase, than by all the powers of natural beauty, of art and history.

To my impression of the blend of medieval and modern dignity in a house that had belonged to Dante's friend, Henry James lent something curiously ineffaceable by gaily adding a touch of our familiar stage-effect. '... I permit you, Lady Paget and her wondrous old Bellosguardo opera-box, as it strikes one, at the spectacle ...' This is the sentence (again to pick up his cue) that has kept the Val d'Arno spread across the memory like a back-drop to the scene.

## CII

*Lamb House, Rye.*
May 20th, 1901

Dear Elizabeth Robins.

How kind and generous, how touching and interesting, your letter, and how deeply I rejoice that you're so soothingly (or soothedly,) and interestingly where you are. Really, nothing, just now, could have

241

given me greater pleasure. It strikes me as absolutely the right thing for you and I hope with all my heart that it will work over you some deep and quiet spell. Florence is the place in the world that I love the best, I think, and I should love it still better, I assure you, if it were to render you the solid service of putting you on your feet. I follow you, I accompany you, everywhere; but I just a little hope for you that the English colony won't tear you too much asunder. The English colony is the dark shade — in a general way — in the picture; and my fondness for the spot of earth is by no means because of them. However, I permit you Lady Paget and her wondrous old Bellosguardo opera-box, as it strikes one, at the spectacle, and I'm very glad Lady Airlie, for whom I've nothing but admiration and affection, has got settled in her nook behind the Spencer Stanhope's — forgive my grotesque writing of that name, which it's too late at night (12.30) to correct. I saw her (Lady A.) last winter just as she was about to start for Florence and I wished her so my benediction that I am delighted the fruit has ripened for her. Stay in Italy as long as you can — don't bolt too soon — try a comfortable Appenine or so if possible; for I venture to believe that your remedy may be in that softly-suffused air if you will only not institute a system of fatal social success. If you could only be, for 3 months, *somewhere,* a quiet social failure, you would become — well, you would become a bloated physical triumph. *Try* it. But it will take a lot of doing — or, rather, of not doing. *Drive* as much as you can, and go to all the old villas you can get into. There are, in one way and another, a great many. I am down here (back again from town these 6 weeks,) till late next autumn, and it's so lovely in England in the wondrous weather we go on having that I can think of Tuscany almost without a pang. I rejoice greatly that you are with Mrs Grosvenor and that she is in Via Venezia. I haven't had a chance to communicate with her for a very long time — and there was a period, for her, when I much wanted to; but I should like at present to send her a very cordial, a tenderly-cordial, greeting. May you be long together, and, strange as the uttered wish sounds, may you be, personally, long away!

Believe me always your devotissimo,

Henry James.


While still suffering from the effects of the typhoid, I wrote from abroad asking advice as to the safest way of dispatching a box from Devonshire to Aix-les-Bains. No common box, yet, judging from Mr. James's letter, I could not have said even so much as that it was heavy, was of wood, was of a size to contain the considerable collection of papers, diary-notes, bundles of letters, several thousand photographs mostly taken by myself; maps; treatises on Arctic-mining and such like material for the rest of that commissioned newspaper work that was to pay back the costs of my journey.

Such intelligence as I could give, now, about

the Klondyke and Alaska had for months been of the kind called with us Piper's News. The last strains of the intoxicating tune 'Arctic Gold' had been piped over the world while I was fighting fever and fighting that worse enemy the doctors call sequelæ.

At Aix I began feebly to hope that out of my box of wreckage, with the help of memory, something might yet be made of the too magnetic north.

But for the thoroughness of Mr. James's intervention the means to that end — the box, would have been lost to any future purpose of the miserable invalid at Aix.

## CIII

*Lamb House,*
*Rye.*

Dear Elizabeth Robins.

I wired you to-day, to save time, on the subject of your Paignton parcels — the parcel-post hence to France now operating beautifully and easily — and the bookpost always. May your documents &c. swiftly and safely reach you — I rejoice more than I can say in the knowledge of your feeling the desire and the faculty for them. This is the good news of your good letter, but it is a delight to hear from you at all. I have to gather from your condensed record that recuperation has kept you company and that you are seeing daylight in your long tunnel. Please believe in the deadly earnestness with which

I watch the enlargement of that bright aperture. It will be a joy to see you again when the wave of recovery does at last wash you up high upon our grassy terra firma. I say 'at last'— but I hope to hear the full music of that beneficent tide by the summer's end. We are having the summer here, as you have doubtless heard, 'neat'— which has been hateful for people in London, but rather bucolic and 'convincing' for those, like myself, in the country. I am sticking fast to this spot, working with a good deal of intensity, praying for rain, putting up relatives, receiving, in a small way, friends (O. W. Holmes — the younger and the actual, is here at this moment;) also wondering much of the time about *you*. I've had a brief correspondence with Mrs Bell and heard of her as the glass of fashion — but in general I've shunned London and all its phantasmagoria as an invention of the Devil. It's something to wait for and live for — the lapful of history and picture that you will, that you *must*, soon — after all — bring back to us; and I feel quite like the first person — the germ of the queue, at the theatre door, before it opens. There will be many behind me, but I hope to get in first. May the Nurse bend tenderly over your Alaskan muse. And may your immersions meanwhile be deep — at Aix — and all your consciousness serene. —

Yours ever so constantly

Henry James

July 31st, 1901.

*Lamb House,*
*Rye.*
Aug. 7th, 1901

Dear Elizabeth Robins.

Your short missive of this a.m. (then received,) has the effect of making me feel miserably stupid in relation to your inquiry of the other day — and I can't now help tearing my hair and cursing my want of wit in your presence — by way of penance and disgrace. I must have wired you, egregiously, what you already knew — whereas what you didn't know — and therefore wanted — was the name of a forwarding agent — which I could instantly have supplied. One has sometimes those fitful abysms — at least *I* have; but why I should have had one *then* — *!* The truth is I was hypnotized — it was a case of suggestion — by some accidental turn in your letter foreshadowing things not of bulk, or of great number — a bundle or two of papers, a blank book or two, and three or four volumes. So I *saw* the articles (and the more fool I!) and so I arranged for them, mentally, as by the quick and easy method of parcel's post, which I have so often used for, and on, the Continent, with advantage. Whereas I could *perfectly* have advised you otherwise if I had only thought of it — and *would,* in that case, have asked you to have the things sent straight to me here, when I myself would easily and safely despatch them. I rage that I didn't do for you that poor thing, and that you had fresh worry and uncertainty in consequence and had to do it all yourself. But I shall rage still worse if you answer this, or take *any notice of it whatever*. It is a mere act of relief to my afflicted spirit. If your box has arrived when my letter reaches you, my earnest prayer will have been sufficiently answered. It is the very devil to me that you are in pain again — but what's the use of Aix then? May it all be past now. Not a *word*, mind, please, of rebuttal of this; only give yourself to your work — your consolation, — and believe your no less stupid than faithful old friend

Henry James

CV

*Lamb House,*
*Rye, Sussex.*
Sept. 6th, 1901

Dear Elizabeth Robins.

It comes over me — at the 11th hour — that I had better, for full co-operation, enclose you this note, though the people do tell me they have written you straight. Let me earnestly beg you to do as they indicate — send the box simply, as a parcel from the Aix-l.-B. railway Station to their care at Dover: whence they will consign it to me here to take care of for you till you want it again. I wish I could be

taking care of *you* instead of your box! Yours, at
any rate, ever so carefully.

Henry James

So it was that in the end I owed to him my
book *The Magnetic North.*

## CHAPTER XIV

# 'KENSINGTON—FLORIDA, FLORIDA—KENSINGTON'

For the first time in twenty-one years Mr. James was in America in 1904-5. He even visited Florida.

Long before this, in England, he had heard my impressions of Hernando County, of the Caloosahatchee and of the great inland sea, Okeechobee, near the Everglades — impressions dating from a time before I first crossed the Atlantic. He had more recently heard about that new Florida Saga referred to in his later letters. I, in my turn, had had to hear unrelenting mockery lavished on my Florida infatuation till, in time, he accepted the hopelessness of my case. The end of his eleven months in America found Mr. James in the summer of 1905 on the point of returning to England. I had come to New York, unexpectedly, on summons by cable to the wedding of my youngest brother. In exchange of news between Mr. James and me, after my arrival, something was said about the bare possibility of my being able, on the shortest of short notices, to get passage back to England on Mr. James's *Ivernia.* It was at the season when all steamers were crammed.

## CVI

Dear Elizabeth Robins.

It breaks my heart that I am till to-morrow p.m. off here in the Massachusetts hills, far from Steamer-offices (and I only found your new letter here last night, on getting back from a two days' motor-absence —) I have only *Monday,* clear, in Boston, to do ALL my last businesses, and I will rush to the Cunard office as soon as I can get in there — from Cambridge, my brother's, after breakfast. But even on the miracle of a cabin *returned* the steamer sails at *10 a.m.* Tuesday, and your margin for reaching B[oston] would be small — though there is a beautiful midnight train from 42nd St. N.Y. that gets there at 7 a.m. Ah, I fear these are vainest dreams — I wish they *mightn't* have been. If I only had let you know sooner, or, rather learned myself sooner, that you were having to turn round for your return so quickly. I am spending 5 days with Mrs Wharton, and this country (the motor helping,) is of admirable beauty; but I am at the end of my long rope — the chord has snapped, and I long for (Sussex) re-patriation. How fain would I converse with you! — and how soon, at the worst, we must manage it! I wince even at learning that you're coming back here in the autumn. How can you? I can tell you, in

London, all about it. But oh for long talks on the deck! Ah, for the miracle!

Yours always

Henry James

The miracle happened. Mr. James was not a specially good sailor but he was far better than I. Few, without being told would have known he was taking a remedy that left him 'dull-witted and drowsy'— though it is true he did not stick very closely to his revision of 'Roderick Hudson.' One reason may have been that among the passengers he had a friend whom he owed, I imagine, to Mrs. Edith Wharton. This was Mr. Walter Berry, an American of cultivated taste and no little personal charm — at home, I understood, in France and in French literature. Some reference was made to a game invented by Mr. Berry and Mrs. Wharton, a game whose name — the Adjective Hunt — sticks in the memory. The lady was the dealer, laying down the latest-written pages of her book. Mr. Berry would take up the challenge, hot on the trail to mark and 'have at' any adjective for whose survival a convincing case could not be made out. Naturally, I looked with respect on the man to whom so distinguished an artist would defer in this mighty matter. Devoted as Henry James was to the Duc de Berry — so he used to call the Walter Berry of the famous suit case [see Lubbock, *Letters of Henry James*] — I cannot imagine Mrs. Wharton's friend, nor any living creature being allowed to question the value of a single specimen of that other part of speech used so lavishly by Henry James. Clearly, no hand but his would

251

have dared touch one of those mettlesome adverbs, which he drove through the mazes on a rein so easy and with so ingenious a mastery.

One or two other 'things heard' come echoing out of that distance. When we had to some extent found our sea-legs and were at the stage of deck-pacing and more connected talk, I was told something about the New America Mr. James had been seeing after the lapse of nearly a quarter of a century. I heard something, too, about his literary plans. The chief one, as it stood in his mind at that moment, was not the Revised Collected Edition. He was committed first of all to do the book of traveller's impressions called *The American Scene*.

I could not help regretting that with such a mass of work in front of him, there would be no possibility of a novel about the New Americans. Perhaps I harped on this unduly, for I remember a touch of impatience in his dismissal of the subject, and then my excitement when he relented and said that a novel about the New Americans was precisely what he was most particularly going to do. But the project was, for the time being, intensely private. To the last degree it was premature so much as to hint at such an idea. For it was not only an idea — it was The Idea. He marvelled that up to now it had so blessedly been let alone. The theme was the immensely increased, the all-but-complete separation of the sexes in modern America. And, upon that, instance after instance illuminating much that had been said before the novel was mentioned. So far, he said, as concerned men's intellectual life, so far as concerned all higher work and most real work of any kind, in every but one relation, a practical divorce between the sexes prevailed. It was a state of segregation beyond anything existing out of the Orient. His novel was to be called *The Chasm*. I don't know if he ever so much as began it. Labours of another sort before and after the years of sickness and deepening depression stretched between him and that other Chasm, the one that opened in 1914.

When I look back to our Atlantic crossing I have the feeling that Mr. James might almost have had a prophetic vision of what lay implicit in the final doom of 'our old *Ivernia*,' as he affectionately called the ship we came to know so well. It was destined to another route and a different errand from bringing him and me safe back to England. Our *Ivernia* was to go shuddering and crashing to the bottom of the Mediterranean with a vast torpedo rent in her side.

Yet all that he said as he stood there, sending that melancholy look of his out over the Atlantic waste, was something by way of friendly protest against this light-minded 'flittering' back and forth between England and America. For 'Chinsegut' had kept coming into the talk in spite of his clear refusal to show any sympathy with my plan of spending the winters in Florida. That delectable region on the unspoiled West Coast, which he had never seen, he had characteristically dismissed in the previous letter with: 'I can tell you in London all about it.'

And now, again, he admonished me. Hadn't I come to the time when I could feel I had adventured enough? The instinct of self-preservation had warned him — didn't it warn me, *'to take in sail . . . ?*

Yet here, too, he was able to show his power of imaginative participation in activities he deplored. 'Morocco' of Manchester Square had long been abandoned. The next letters covered what Mr. James called 'the Kensington-Florida, Florida-Kensington period.'

## CVII

*Lamb House,*
*Rye,*
*Sussex.*

September 25th, 1905

Dear Elizabeth Robins.

It does me good, the greatest, to hear from you and to know you are soon to be accessible in town. I rejoice in the prospect of seeking you out on the very 1st occasion that I am 'up' long enough to turn round. There are various prospects of this — of a few flying visits during the autumn — and I will make sure of you, very gratefully, in advance, for the earliest favouring date. That *may* be a date about October 10th — I will earnestly work it out. What wonderful wanderings you must have been having (I thirst for the detail of the same,) and how grandly you play with life — I mean to such tunes as your Kensington-Florida and your Florida-Kensington. You will be having fine homesicknesses at the one for the other, and fine leaps and bounds from the other to the one! It will really be a grand sporting existence for you, and I'm too glad to happen to be contemporary (for a fraction) with the spectacle of it! Do you know your Southern (that is Floridian, purely) details make *me* homesick? and I'm not sure that a more intimate command of them wouldn't make me bolt (hence) altogether. *I* shouldn't come back. Therefore it's lucky for me that I haven't the solicitation. Please commend me very kindly to the Bells — I send them my love, without a grain of reservation, my 'best'— and think very desiringly of seeing *them* in town, too, on one of my later incursions. I want to try to be able to go with you to one of the 'Vedrenne &c.' * performances, and am yours very constantly.

Henry James

The identity of C. E. Raimond with E. R. had been made known by a mischance. My novel-writing might now be called an established habit, but for the fact that it was not so very established, and was not even consistently a habit. Still, there it was, and there was Mr. James ready to do what he could about it.

CVIII

*The Reform Club*
March 28th, 1906

Dear Elizabeth Robins.

I have perforce failed of going to 95 Sloane St. this evening — where my one design and hope would

---

* The reference is to a remarkable series of plays done under Vedrenne-Barker management, an enterprise which showed Granville-Barker to be the Master-producer of the English-speaking world. His retirement from this field left a blank no one has ever filled.

have been to have some talk with you. This possibility I have dallied with — but I have been frustrated of it, and I console myself with being sure that I should have been buffetted, in fact by 10 other people, and you beguiled away by 20 others, and I shouldn't have got anything of you at all. I have succumbed, very weary-weary and worn to the necessity (after a tangled day) of going to bed very early (though it's now 11.15!) — as I've not dined out. Accordingly I scrawl here, pointedly, one of the things I should have said to you a word about if we *had* met. I saw my very valuable friend and 'literary agent' this afternoon, and he broke ground to me on the subject of the hope he had long entertained of having the privilege of 'acting' for you in respect to your books. Did I not sometimes see you, and if so might I possibly not mention to you that this hope always burns within his breast, I am (as I immediately told him I should be) delighted to mention it to you, and I don't wait till I see you to say so — but find myself really quite *impatient* to say it. He has been so extraordinarily helpful to me, and I find him in every way so efficient and ingenious and honourable and prompt and wise, that, an opportunity given, I can't *not* testify. He has transformed my situation little by little about which I had been idiotically helpless myself. He has just arranged a very complex and difficult job for me in a masterly way — the matter of a 'handsome' collective (and *se*lective) Edition Définitive of my writings, in the U.S. and here — a tiresome worrying business through the scatterment of my books through a number of publishers, who were all to be triumphantly dealt with. He has so dealt and made the thing possible — I couldn't have *touched* it by myself. But I only wanted to mention a title or so for him, in my eyes — since I am thus speaking for him. (This affair of the Edition, by the bye, please, is very private and confidential.) If you *are* thinking of him, *do* think of him — and I will tell you as much more as you like. But let it not be prejudicial to my seeing you very soon — I will come to you — as soon as you get back to Iverna Gardens?? Chilworth St. seems a bit complicated to yours very constantly

Henry James

P.S. Don't acknowledge this — or if you perversely will, do it only by 3 words in pencil! Don't I know — ????

! ! ! ! ! !

(This represents a whirlwind.)

## CHAPTER XV

# VOTES FOR WOMEN

Mr. James had heard from me that I wanted to talk over my rough draft of a play dealing with Militant Suffrage. A number of letters passed and several meetings were entirely devoted to this congenial subject!

## CIX

*Lamb House,*
*Rye,*
*Sussex.*

Nov. 9th, 1906

Dear Elizabeth Robins.

Your note this morning received appeals to me intensely and almost makes me howl with the wish that I had a little more *immediate* freedom. My head and imagination are full of my own current and urgent imagery and issues, and it won't be till I can clear it, alas, that I can do *much*. But very earnestly will I meanwhile do what I *can*, and very interestedly, and however limpingly and clumsily.

258

But I *must* look at the play as it stands again — and I wired you this a.m. to ask if I mayn't read over Act I. I ought to have asked for them *all* — just to *re*-read. I read it but once. You shall have it straight back; with *every* suggestion I can gouge out. What I want to do is to *dictate,* for you, in type, some groping ghost of a Scenario. But my amanuensis is away till *Tuesday.* But after Tuesday! And meanwhile I shall have re-perused — re-meditated.

Always yours

Henry James

## CX

*Lamb House,*
*Rye,*
*Sussex.*

Nov. 24, 1906

My dear E.R.

Very interesting your news and pungent as the smoke of battle sniffed from afar off — to a captive warrior. Don't be afraid I don't understand (or shouldn't, on seeing it,) every (or any) development or trait the closer working out of your scheme imposes on you as you go. My indications have a possible worth as tentative, elastic, plastic only — made to be adjusted, to be arranged and fitted, and *certain,* I felt, to have to be re-handled. And I see perfectly what you meant about Miss L.* — *who will*

* Miss L. is Veda Lovering the chief woman's part in the Suffrage play.

*take more playing that way;* but who becomes the more interesting, I am sure and about your idea of whom &c. I was a good deal in the dark when I made those very provisional notes (through not having talked with you about her.) To write thus is for me really to want to *see* it all again — and to talk a bit more and to keep on a little with you. Should you — *shall* you — be in London on Tuesday 4th?? I shall have to be there — probably for that night only — and that day. I could probably put in 3 or 4 days — over Act 4th — *after* the 6th, 8th, or thereabouts. Make me some sign if there is anything in this for you. I'm sorry to hear you've been at all 'low'— on such heights. But I congratulate you heartily on the stiff back you present to your benighted manageress. Keep *that* up and all else will come right. I'm kind of glad I've no *Bell* — not even *one,* of the apparently several different sorts. But I greet all the sorts for their goodness to you (and Sir Hugh for everything) and am yours always

Henry James

'Votes for Women' had been accepted for immediate production by the Vedrenne-Barker management of the Court Theatre — with the woman I most wanted, Miss Wynne-Matheson, in the principal part. It was a great moment.

*Lamb House,*
*Rye,*
*Sussex.*

March 5th, 1907

Dearest E.R.! (for nothing but the superlative meets the case)

How perfectly delightful and adorable and how absolutely and as it *should* be! It's the one and only way in which the Play should be presented: anything less was, all the while, a most 'fell' (indeed!) and inferior pis-aller, I almost weep for joy; I congratulate you to extravagance; and I lose myself in the vision of how interesting and inspiring and triumphant the whole business is now going to be for you! The only heartbreak is (for there's always one *somewhere* when anything good turns up,) that I go abroad hideously to-morrow, for some eight or ten weeks — and shall be far just when I should have yearned to be nearest! This is really damnable — it poisons my departure. I should even have dreamed of seeing a rehearsal. As it is I shall see only the swing of the run. *My* run — to get back and see — will be as swinging! How jolly and interesting to have Granville Barker — an intelligence and a competence so great — to work with! My blessings on him and the heroic (as they will have to be,) rehearsals! I take for granted Miss McCarthy for Bea, but I seem to see — or to hear — that is to fear

261

— X ——'s thin patter for Miss L. and that's another affair. I lose myself in the rest — Barker to be Geoffrey?? — and I shan't know anything only burst in ignorance unless some day when rehearsals are going you find some leisure, some off-moment, on the stage, to scrawl me in pencil on a scrap of paper, the Cast — and your feelings — and as much else as possible. Anything *here* instantly forwarded. At any rate Angels and Ministers of Grace defend you! Yours more than ever

Henry James

P.S. *What* you must have been through!

## CXII

*58 rue de Varenne.*
*Paris*
April 13th, 1907

Dear Elizabeth Robins.

Your deeply interesting note overtook me three days since while plunged in a prodigious three-weeks motor-tour (over half France;) from which I returned only last night to pens and ink and breathing-time. Immensely interesting your news [of Granville-Barker's production of the play 'Votes for Women'] — but I couldn't pray for you as I had it (your letter) a day too late! Still, I am praying now — as hard as one can pray in so much darkness and remoteness and uninformedness (*that* is what I mean.) I feel 'out of it', dreadfully and sorely, here, and don't see the notices, have missed the journals, and have no means of knowing how your First 'went' to all appearance. But I shall make that up, by hook and crook, tooth and nail — for I *ache* with interest, sympathy, curiosity. With all my heart I hope for happy and comfortable things. Is there any report you could most beneficently and mercifully *send* me? It would be crystal water in the desert to yours tout-dévot

Henry James

## CXIII

*58 Rue de Varenne.*
*Paris.*
May 1st, 1907

My dear E.R.

I don't know why — or rather I do! — I have so basely delayed to thank you for the newspaperisms about the Play of which you the other day so obligingly sent me a sheaf. I say I do know, because Paris is, from day to day — for a voyage of some weeks — a great vessel in which one is so shaken about that one can scarcely cling to the table and the chair long enough to work the necessary pen. But, at any rate, even through these poverties and vulgarities of reportership I seem to make out the impression made by the performed thing — and above all by the 2nd Act — which I feel it deplorable that I have missed. The Protheros have been here, very briefly, however, and it's from dear Fanny of that ilk that I've extracted the vividest sense that the whole thing holds, moves its audience powerfully. Her tribute to this was eloquent and she again made me squirm with regret. Therefore why the Devil don't they put you on in the evening — if the notice of 'last two (day) performances' that I see in the *D. Telegraph* means that they don't? What an abyss of treachery the theatre — again and unfailingly? I don't return to England till about June 15th, but do keep the story fresh and fair for yours ever so yearningly

Henry James

## CHAPTER XVI

# PROFESSOR WILLIAM JAMES

The reference in the next letter is to an old idea of mine to write a novel dealing with the problems of the Negro in America. This I presumptuously hoped to do from the Negro's point of view. My old knowledge of the uneducated would naturally have to be reinforced by some new acquaintance with the educated coloured people.

When he commended me to the hospitality of his brother, Henry James did more for me than he could have dreamed — more, I mean, in enlarging my immediate outlook, though I am far from meaning only that.

The visit to Professor and Mrs. William James (and it is not often that two people can be thought of so easily as one) remains one of the later American landmarks I care most to remember. No less at that time than in the retrospect those days and nights in Irving Street, of the Harvard precincts, justified and enriched my sense of American values.

I have in my day heard a good deal of good

265

talk. I never heard better than in William James's study. There is little need to say the subjects were by no means restricted to the field of my special interest at the moment. Yet, as to that, I could not have gone to any man in America better able to enlighten me than precisely Henry James's brother. He knew what was open to a white man to know about Negroes in the North. He had recently made a lecture tour throughout the part of the United States that used to be called the Black Belt. Prof. James had not only addressed instructors and students in the coloured colleges and schools: he had taken his turn at listening to his hosts, and talking with them in private. Knowing, as I naturally did, something about the life and work of the chiefs of the two sections of Negro leadership (Booker Washington and Burghardt du Bois) the facts told me by William James were less surprising than his interpretation of the facts. In all the discussions of this problem of the American future, which had ranged — and raged — through my youth, and that deepened and widened as the years went on, I had never heard any one speak of Negro education and our common future with such sympathy, understanding, and such courage as Professor James.

I cannot think how I escaped attacking the theme unless it was through that better knowledge of its complexity and gravity that I owed to Henry James's distinguished brother.

# CXIV

November 10th, 1907

My dear E.R. and most Indescribable of Women!

This is intensely interesting and awfully prodigious — and I congratulate you with all my heart on so honourable a call and a job so worthy of your powers and so amenable to your experience! I feel that altogether the best thing for me to do will be to send you a letter to my Brother William at Cambridge — for he can tell you in 10 minutes more of the matter and whom to know and see (he knows Jerome for instance much better than I do — I don't know him much) than certain others could probably do in 10 hours. (I think you already met him — years ago — in your old 'Compton'— 1st night of 'American' &c. days.) He will be of very good counsel and of large suggestion — the subject interests him highly — and Booker Washington, Du Bois &c are his Intimates! But you must *see* him, talk with him (you'll be in Boston, surely?) *not* deal with him only by letter. I will — beside writing separately to my brother — send you my missive before you wonderfully sail.

Yours all and always

Henry James

## CXV

My dear E.R.

Here is the letter to my Brother, my dear E.R. —
delayed only because of late I have been having a
hell of a time (con rispetto parlando,) and letters
have suffered, at my hands, discourtesy no less
inevitable than abominable. I won't go into details
— but you can 'take' it from me. But this now carries
you my very cordial benediction. If you don't find
my Brother interesting, responsive, suggestive, helpful, human all in the very highest degree — well,
hold me responsible and I will somehow otherwise
make it up to you. But that never happened to any
one. He is wholly at home now — it is his time for
being so, and he has work that keeps him there.
And my sister in law, though fatigued and over-
done, is a pearl of price — I recommend her to you,
on *knowledge*. I follow you forth in a wondering
and awe-stricken spirit — wonder and awe being now
the more emphasised than ever notes of all the admiration and affection with which you inspire me.
You'll probably have a more interesting time than
any mere woman is properly entitled to — rapidly as,
by your care, her titles are rising. I fondly hope, and
seem to make out, that by the time you return I
shall be settled in town for a while. That all ease and

268

honour may attend you is the prayer of your faith-
fullest old friend

Henry James

December 2nd, 1907

## CXVI

My dear Elizabeth R.

I have two good letters from you, and rejoice in
each; but have been pre-occupied and *immersed* beyond power of response till this moment. I came
back last night — by which I mean I arrived this
a.m. — from a tussle with the Black Devil of the
Theatre at Edinburgh and elsewhere (for dingy
'tour' rehearsals,) and only now am breathing again
after an apparently happy issue (on Thursday
night,) of my adventure. The Edinburgh production
of the little piece ['The High Bid'] has been to all
seeming, quite a Victory over possible *provincial*
mischance — and I hope greatly the thing will
eventuate here, somewhere, in May. But I trust
(though I am still most impermanent,) that I shall
see you long before that. What you told me of your
little time with my Brother and his wife quite
ravished me with satisfaction — I *knew* some good
would come to you of them. They *probably* come
out to lecture at Oxford in May. I find myself here
— after a sleepless night in the Scotch Express —
face to face with a mountain of letters that I've had
to neglect while mumming — so this is all now save

the most explicit and affectionate welcome back. Your great globe-oscillations excite the wonder, pity, terror, rapture of yours all constantly

Henry James

Reform Club, S.W.
    March 28th, 1908


## CXVII

*3 Place des Etats Unis,*
*Paris*
April 29th, 1908

My dear E.R.!

I am thrilled by the interest of your letter and most yearningly with you in spirit, but see where I am in the flesh (spending 14 days here with Mrs. Wharton — of which but 4 or 5 have expired). I return to England on the 9th (D.V.) and shall be in London from the 11th May to about a similar date in June. Shall you not soon be in town again — or if at Blythe couldn't I come to see you *there?* Or does the question (of the best function — or office — of your subject) press so that it can't conveniently wait? It's a kind of question that interests me immensely at all times — and would reach — would make — the maximum of appeal to me as communicated by you. (I do think the kinds of subjects for novel and play essentially differ.) But do let me hear from you that you *have* to be in town a little in May. I should so immensely like to discourse of the matters with you. My brother and his wife are due at Liverpool (in our old *Ivernia*) this very day and he gives 8 'Hibbert' Lectures at Oxford at the rate of 2 a week I suppose. I shall go from town to such as I can. Won't you go to one *with* me? Do at any rate — give me more news of the great *Idea*. I immensely long to see you. Yours always

Henry James

## CXVIII

*Reform Club,*
*Pall Mall, S.W.*
May 12th, 1908

Dear Elizabeth Robins.

Monday 25th will do beautifully and I will communicate with you further about it. I rejoice greatly that you are so favourably moved to the little pilgrimage. I go on Thursday next (I came back from Paris but on Sunday and from Rye but yesterday) — and know as yet but that the lectures *are* on Thursdays and Mondays. I feel confident they will go on over the 25th — but will bring back with me *all* knowledge. I'm only disconcerted at having to wait so many days for your 'subject.' I adore subjects — and it's a strain. However, I feel sure I shall be repaid. And I shall tell you on my side of one of the strangest (and most revealing) experiences possible — the dress rehearsal the other night in Paris of

271

the very literal French version of B.S.'s 'Candida.' Revealing of so many things — of which I shan't be able however to tell you half. But I shall write again. Yours always

Henry James

## CXIX

The Reform Club,<br>Pall Mall, S.W.

My dear E.R.

At the same moment I return from several hours at Oxford (my brother's 4th lecture, but the 1st I've heard,) I get your letter. I am sorry to say that I fear it turns out rather well — for a particular reason — that you doubt being able to go on the 25th. My brother, I found to my sorrow — though I knew it more or less — is unwell, very nervously so — so that he is just pulling through his course of seven (he's obliged to give up one,) by the skin of his teeth. He has to take such precautions, lie down, do no talking and generally abstain from any sort of contact the day he lectures that he could scarcely even see me at all, and I passed my time mostly with my sister-in-law. He rises to the scratch, at the hour, and the lecture was beautifully given, but the effect of to-day's impression has been to make me give up the idea (which I had had) of going to next Thursday's and the following Monday's (or rather vice versa). I shall probably go down on Monday the

25th, for that will be the last — but my conviction is that if you should, or *could* go, you would find the pleasure of the thing impaired by his hampered and hindered state. Therefore don't regret that you have to give it up. I am convinced he will be better after the business is over and the anxiety relaxed; but he isn't fit, really, to have come out on so arduous a job — and must (and will) give up hereafter everything of the sort. They will be in London, I hope and trust, for a little, toward the end of the month, or early in June, and they have the greatest desire to see you again. But at this rate — ???? Do you, *don't* you, come up at all? How then otherwise am I to hear your story? — for which I pine. Do find something possible. I am here all this month — and a little later.

Yours all faithfully

Henry James

May 14th, 1908.

## CHAPTER XVII

# ILLNESS AND
# 'BACK TO WORK'

As much of the time from 1907 onward as found me in England, I was living in the country, making occasional short visits to London, and seeing less of my older friends. In the year 1908 Mr. James was going through the final stages of what he called 'the Nightmare of the Edition,' that considerable revision and careful editing of twenty-four volumes of his collected works — a gigantic task which I so incongruously see him 'at,' not a groaning worker before a groaning table at Rye, but with 'Roderick Hudson' lightly in hand lolling, yes, positively lolling, at length in a steamer chair on a sunlit deck at sea. The most valuable part of the work for the collected edition (as well as most costly to him), the Prefaces, must come to stand, I believe, for very much what he hoped, or will so stand when they are made accessible in a single volume. 'They ought, collected together,' he wrote Mr. W. D. Howells, 'to form a sort of a comprehensive manual or vade-mecum for aspirants in our arduous profession.'

This vast labour of the final edition was com-

274

plicated by ill-health. He was writing about himself already in 1908, as 'a stopped clock,' and though he was so far from approaching that condition, he was saying early in the autumn of 1909 that he would never be quite the same after the heart attack he had suffered from a year earlier.

## CXX

*Lamb House,*
*Rye,*
*Sussex.*
November 15th, 1908

Dear Elizabeth Robins.

Ah, how I wish I *could!* But I am far off — though with London tugging at me all the time, to my ruin and confusion — and this time going up is, alas, heartbreakingly impossible. With all of which I never, in these days, see you, and it can't go on, and it shan't, and I shall do something — but *now* I can only be all helplessly and woefully — just because I am all devotedly — yours,

Henry James

## CXXI

*Lamb House,*
*Rye.*
May 9th, 1909

Dear Elizabeth Robins.

What a dumb ungracious brute you must think me!

Your kind note came wandering down here *after*

the occasion as to which you generously wrote me and found me so demoralized by a particular pressure (which had helped a recurrent torment of shoeless gout to drive me, for peace and safety, from town,) that a complete loss of head, and almost of heart, in respect of my correspondence simply and shamelessly imposed itself. I am in the all-else blighting predicament of the feverish finish of a belated Book (by May 20th) — a book doubly belated by the untoward accident of my winter, which punched in my Time a vast gaping Hole, — four-fifths of it are set up and printed and waiting ferociously for my now solemnly promised remainder (so that the book may be out by July 1st,) and I have surrendered myself as regards everything else to abysses of ineptitude. I am, when my daily stint is done, so spent and finished and voided of all matter of articulation, that this is the sort of letter I write when I write any. Forgive it, please, and cast over it the mantle of your charity. To make up for it I'll send you the book. It's delightful to me to gather that you're again in the bill. This means, I trust, that you are wholly well. But the pen drops from my hand and I am yours no less wearily than constantly

Henry James

P.S. I do intensely intend to be in town again when my job is finished. Then I shall reach out to you.

The 'so jolly-well entitled play' was probably Lady Bell's 'The Way the Money Goes.'

# CXXII

My dear E.R.

The day before I so fallaciously dreamed (for ½ an hour) that I might have figured on your brilliant scene I tumbled back into bed, very dismally — to a fresh — a 5th — collapse after a presumptuous and premature push forward. I have been in fine dismally and drearily ill — but am again sitting up and feeling pretty confidently better — though it's yet but the confidence of the last 36 hours. And life reasserts itself to the tune of my wishing immensely I might have been going with you to Florence Bell's so jolly-well *entitled* play — which I hope with all my heart has had — or will have — the happiest, pleasantest fate. I wrote her a poor little word a few days ago — so please kindly mention better news of me. To me too Edward Grey 'says' much more than Asquith — but I lie here verily as detached as a sick god on a damp Olympus — in a dark deep hollow, however, and far from the summit. As soon as I am at all (or *very*) firm on my feet I shall come up to town and thence down to tea with you. I assume your consent, and thank you for all your fidelity and am most all-faithfully yours

Henry James

277

Henry James did not shut out his friends from participation even in illness. The letters that follow are no mere statement of the prime fact, or of the outer effects and final results of illness, but give one leave to come near to his unimaginable suffering.

After the worst was over in his own case, he was to go on pilgrimage with his dying brother.

## CXXIII

*Grand Hotel*
*Beau-Rivage*
*Genève*
June 8th, 1910

My dear and generous old friend!

How kind and beautiful your letter to me from Dresden, and what a tender spirit of friendship moved you to write it! It finds me here on my way back to England after a few weeks in these neighbouring (roughly speaking) parts with my brother and sister-in-law. I came abroad with them (first to Bad-Nauheim for *him* — not profitably I fear;) but the whole bedrenched incident will soon have closed and I shall on Aug. 12th go with them for several months to America. Since that weird moment of our meeting, weeks and weeks ago, in the dim theatre-box many troubled things have happened — most of all that I had straight thereafter a miserable aggravation of my state of health and nerves on

WILLIAM JAMES

realizing which they came as ministering angels out to me: I was wholly unfit to be alone, and in terror of being so. Then followed a black bad time (of horrible nervous illness and melancholia) over which I drop the veil. I am emerging, but must make a long absence from my solitary home, and they offer me (over there) infinite hospitality, affection and protection. And there are many urgent motives for my going — so I go; and it will probably be for some 9 or 10 months. I shall be (with them) in London between the last days of this month and Aug. 10th — and would come to you in the country for luncheon (that is I *think* I should be able to,) should you be back there then. I thank you more than I can say for your delightful, moving references to all the dear old things and associations of the past. Ah the pleasure of seeing you again! Any word to *Rye* always reaches your ever-devoted

Henry James

P.S. And now I *forget* your country local name (address) and have to try otherwise.

## CXXIV

*Lamb House,*
*Rye,*
*Sussex.*
July 26th, 1910

Dear Elizabeth Robins.

Your very kind letter only renews my sense, alas, of the difficulties of my situation. We returned from

the Continent ten days ago, I very much more on
the road to be more or less *well* again, but my poor
dear brother in a very aggravated state of the heart
trouble under the cloud of which we all three were
when I wrote. We came down here 4 days ago —
after a very anxious and pre-occupied week in London, and he is so weak and ill and *down,* and has
dropped so rapidly further, that all our anxiety now
is to help him to strength to sail for home by Aug.
12th, for which all his and my sister's and my own
arrangements are made. He must rest here quietly
and under intense care, and his state is such, and
the complications for my sister-in-law so great, that
I fear I can't *plan* for any absence — they are too
sorely on my mind, and the weakness of my own
not entire recovery from the ordeal of these 7
months, makes anxieties come hard for me. So how,
alas, can I definitely say, now, that I will come to
you? I *fear* I shall not be able to leave this place
for a day at all — till the eve of our sailing. And
you go away next week — and the thing looks (as
things are now for us here at this juncture,) so difficult as to be impossible. I deeply regret it — a visit
to you would do me good, the greatest. But I am
really too worried and too sensible of worry in my
own as yet imperfectly redeemed state. I bless you
for your dear benevolence of thought. We shall meet
in happier conditions — not *too* long hence, I feel.
But all the present and all the recent past (of this
year) are dark and tormenting — to yours none the

less affectionately and intendingly, and, in time, sur-
mountingly,

Henry James

## CXXV

Dear Elizabeth Robins.

I received, on my beloved Brother's death a very
tender and faithful word from you; but the days
have been heavy with me, I have sat in darkness
and infinitely stricken (also with a flood of kind
letters to acknowledge,) and these poor belated
words are the result. Great has been the woe of all
these last months — with its tragic climax, and great
the dislocation of my life. But I am emerging from
the worst of it (in my own personal case,) and see
a little better where I am. Where I am in the more
immediate sense is with my sister in law and her
children — to whom I am devoted and with and
near whom I shall spend the next three or four
months. I doubt even whether I shall be in a state
or of a disposition to return to England before the
early summer. However, I forbear from plans —
and content myself with howling home-sickness for
the county of Surrey [Sussex] and other parts well
known to us! If I hadn't weighty reasons, and they
(that is my sister, nephews and niece) weren't so
divinely good to me here, I should give up the effort
— that is should yield to the impossibility — of loving this our country *on* the spot. I should still be

willing to do what I can at a distance — however, I will some day, on the nearest day in fact — tell you more. I am slowly getting back to work * — after nearly 2 years' impossibility of *that* — and this greatly helps. I think of *your* conditions — those I seem to see about you — as ideal and unattainable bliss — and I am yours all affectionately

Henry James

95 Irving St.
    Cambridge, Mass. U.S.A.

Oct. 30, 1910

Written from his Sussex home, to me in my Sussex home, during one of his last flights further afield than Oxford.

CXXVI

*Caledonian Hotel,*<br>
*Edinburgh*<br>
Sept. 24th, 1911

My dear old friend!

Your good letter has come after me by devious ways, overtaking me here where I have drawn breath for a couple of nights on my way back from a friend's sequestered (so far as anything is sequestered to-day,) grouse-moor in Forfarshire. I have been at Lamb House but one week since my return from America early in August and have spent a

---

\* To those incomparable and beloved volumes 'A Small Boy and Others' and 'Notes of a Son and Brother.'

month in 4 or 5 other places. I return home on Wednesday 27th, and I sadly gather that this represents an inevitable postponement of the great pleasure of coming over to you (before the 30th) as you beautifully propose. The case is this — that, save for that week just named and 10 days in Aug. 1910 I have been absent from my household gods without the least break for 14 months, and that when I shall have crossed my threshold a few days hence I fear the influences there will make it difficult for me to plan another *immediate* flight. I shall collapse — lie flat — cling somehow to my doorposts. But I greatly, very greatly, long to see you again, and will make the pilgrimage, with all fidelity, as soon as you are so good as to make me a sign that you are back from your own absence. I yearn for an acquaintance with your Sussex setting — I hear it's so admirable — and above all I yearn for a renewal of you; so long and so unnaturally defeated. I shall perhaps miss the blooming Boy * — but we must, he and I, make that up. Let me at any rate count on some brave October day? — mayn't I? — and believe me all affectionately yours

Henry James

To end these 'Participations,' of his I go from the previous letter to one dating more than ten years earlier.

This 'flittering back' and forth through time

* David Scott, author, twenty years later, of that "classic of deep-sea diving," *Seventy Fathoms Deep*.

is against all the canons. I have no better excuse for my irregularity than my own comfort in taking leave of these letters with the one that invoked his blessing after my longest journey — the blessing he sent out to meet my return from the Klondyke.

## CXXVII

*Lamb House,*
*Rye,*
September 25th, 1900

My dear Elizabeth Robins.

I grasp the first free moment since the sorry news, the melancholy, miserable, most distressing news, reached me of your grave illness — but on the heels of it, most blessedly too, the tidings of your apparent victory, your turn for the better, your promise (I hope assured beyond all wavering by the time you get this) of a straight and masterful convalescence. Let these poor words serve as a sign of how troubled, how absorbed and vivid, how almost haunting a vision it has all given me of you — lighting up with its sudden lurid glow the obscurity that closed over you, to my eyes, (not to be till three or four days ago in any degree lifted) from the hour I took leave of you on that last hurried London glimpse. I've been myself obscure, wholly buried here, and (save for a concatenation of family presences, complications and contacts) sightless and soundless of any source of information about you. I've had to forge and fashion it all for myself, and I confess (familiar with processions of evil as my base mind is) that I've fashioned it to a somewhat melancholy tune. I've been — I won't pretend to anything else — abjectly, consistently, magnificently anxious about you. Never, then, was a man more admirably justified. I've spared you literally nothing and now I get it all back. Mrs Bell and Heinemann, however, have given me but scraps and crumbs — so that my own rich gift of evocation finds almost as much as ever to its hand. It continues, out of its materials, to colour the picture. All one can do, as one sits before it, is to chatter to you thus vainly and feebly — as an aid to the ease of one's nerves. I think of you, I watch with you, I pray for you — all with an extreme intensity of tenderness. If these deep agitations of faraway friends could breathe upon your troubled case, how beatified (I mean how *more* than instantly relieved and uplifted,) you would promptly become! I doubt if it has been given to many women in this prosaic age (so far as the age of your adventures *can* be prosaic!) to unite so many of the scattered (the even disunited) in a communion of attention and emotion. Well, don't tell me that we're *not* pulling you, by our monstrous, our helpless alliance, smoothly and steadily through. I say 'Don't tell me,' as if you really could tell me anything. If you only *could* tell me *what* you could — or merely three words of it — it would be just now the miracle that would most convert me. But I launch this little fragile vessel of remembrance and affection upon the deep and into the darkness. I put into the bottle thus cast overboard mere babbled hopes — as a sign. I hope you are not despoiled of the essential elements, I hope you have had revelations of humanity and fidelity. I hope your convalescence, by the time you renounce the attempt to decipher this, will have set in with all the indispensable rigour. I hope, above all, that in confirmation of this I shall right soon receive from Mrs Bell, to whom I've addressed a petition that would melt a heart of stone, some token that she has had a direct word from you. When this befalls I shall unscrupulously write to you again. I daresay you will feel even now that I have addressed you but an empty manifesto — newsless and uninforming. But that I *have* no news is really almost a joy to me, so dangerous a commodity has that become to deal with — beside which I somehow feel that our domestic twaddle may all affect you (with strange fierce scenes and glooms and glories in your eyes,) as ignoble and even incredible. I've stirred no step from this all summer — and 'this' is of a mild and merciful flatness —! However, after all, you may, you must, you *do*, re-hunger and re-thirst for the decent little island. We've had a mainly scorching summer and a simply divine September. But, again, I blush for my twaddle. So, simply, believe that I cherish the dream of your restoration and return, and that I am, dear Elizabeth Robins, more than ever yours,

Henry James

## CHAPTER XVIII

# AT THE LAST

The latest letters of all, received mostly while I was out of England, are not available now. Some of them were dated from Carlyle Mansions. But I never 'see' Mr. James so clearly there, where I saw him last, as I see him in that earlier place where he wrote most of 'The Tragic Muse,' and so much that followed, 'by a wide west window that, high aloft, looked over near and far London sunsets ... or the good fog-filtered Kensington mornings.' * The De Vere Gardens setting had seemed his proper London frame, with the ceremonious old butler at the door admitting to a length of hall and leading on to book-furnished, picture-hung spaces and a dining-room of a special plenished dignity.

I have called on my old friend at the beginning to strike the note of this book. To end it I would like to bring the intention of my faithful echo. The key is the enduring quality in such relationship. Its power of survival seems to owe less to volition than to inevitability, for it needs no reminding and no fostering. In spite of dissimilarity

* Preface to The Tragic Muse.

— or because of it — in the teeth of every kind of inequality, here is an instance (speaking of course for myself alone) where mind turns to mind with a sense of enhancement in the act of sharing.

After being for months away, in Florida or wherever, something would happen or be heard that cried out for the special audience that was Henry James, for the mind that would miss no faintest undertone, the eye that would see more in the scene than any other. Without Henry James's 'assistance' this thing, whatever it might be, fine, or gay or poignant, would lack some precious element of fineness, drollery or apprehended Fate. In such a relationship there is something, I cannot but think, as nearly indestructible as comes to mortals. It accepts absence, change — and is itself unchanged.

One instance of this comes back clearly, through the darkness of the war. In the vast preoccupations of that time we did not often meet. But I knew of his passionate participation there, and I knew of his private service. I knew, of course, of his public testimony. In addition to Mr. James's major reason for taking such a step, he shared in those that weighed on others. All of us, not of British birth, felt the harsh pressure of the stigma Alien; felt the incongruity of police supervision over lovers of England; felt in the business of finger-print-taking a bewildered approach to the criminal class, and suffered the check to eager service through that requirement 'to report' each time, before one could go from an established home in the country to do one's modest war-work in London. The necessity of it all was clear and had to be borne with what patience we could find.

To some of us, not least of the elements of unreality in the situation was the simple faith, on the part of all Governments, that to recite a formula and to write down one's name, could really change nationality. In Mr. James's becoming a British subject there was a significance that belonged solely to himself, a significance that did him honour and, as one feels, did England honour, too. I cannot think that even those carrying the vast burden of British policy, or any soldier at the front, was more penetrated by the influences of the war than Henry James. The stupendous tragedy haunted, obsessed, racked him. As Mr. Lubbock finely says: 'His spiritual vigour bore a strain that was the greater by the whole weight of his towering imagination. . . .'

Though I did not fully realize how ill he had been, I knew he was still too weak to be seen before I crossed the Atlantic the second time during those first eighteen months of the war. I have no recollection of writing him, however briefly, what must (the moment he was better) have had its interest for Henry James, bearing as it did on the one and only theme. For the time was that intensely critical hour in the international politics of 1916 when the fortunes of the Allies had sunk, and when the insoluble problem of Contraband and Blockade threatened a break between England and America. Henry James was one of the first to feel that if the United States really sympathized with the Allies, she could not be standing outside watching them bleed to death. Not only in Europe but in America President Wilson was spoken of as pro-German. His emissary, Colonel House, was in London at the moment after a third visit to Berlin. Many a mind besides Henry James's had been torn with dread lest the splendour of the Kaiser's Court and the paraded might of the German Army would send the simple private citizen back to Washington with a report of the invincibility of German power.

So it was much in those days to know that friendly relations were still maintained between the British Foreign Office and President Wilson's personal agent. Ignorant as I was, I knew that all essentials in the situation would ultimately reach Mr. James through the American Embassy, but I felt that the comfortable assurance had come to me in a form sure to appeal to him.

It came during luncheon with Sir Edward Grey, a couple of days before I sailed for New York in the *New Amsterdam*. 'That's the steamer,' he said, 'that House is going by.' He took for granted I should be seeing something of Colonel House. When I said I had never met him: 'But you will, on board ship. And you will like him.' Though I knew how little chance there was of my being given the opportunity to prove this, Sir Edward Grey's tone of friendliness toward Colonel House had its comfort.

Few people knew, then, what must never be forgotten — that at a time when, the world over, war passion was at its hottest the British Minister for Foreign Affairs kept his Peace-mind. If Sir Edward Grey was not the first to invent the phrase that was to make history, he had written to President Wilson, via Colonel House, as long ago as the previous August: 'the pearl of great price, if it can be found, would be some League of Nations. . . .' Six weeks later, Sir Edward was pressing his point far beyond any mere intervention in *this* war. 'To me,' he wrote Colonel House, 'the great object of securing the elimination of militarism and navalism is to get security for the future against aggressive war.'

Ignorance on the part of ordinary people about these momentous Anglo-American discussions, may be measured by the fact that at a time when Colonel House was spending long hours daily at the British Foreign Office, Sir Francis Bertie, the Ambassador in Paris, sent Sir Edward Grey a dispatch telling him President Wilson's agent, House, was in London and advising Sir Edward to get into touch with him!

But this had been months ago. The situation had grown darker and infinitely more embittered. By the beginning of 1916, Germans in responsible quarters were prey to deep anxiety as to the effect of English influence on President Wilson's Representative. During the next months a desperate effort would be made by each of the belligerent groups, and Colonel House was returning home to advise the President on which side America should come in! It was known that when Colonel House was recently in Berlin the *Tageblatt* reported his saying: 'Each time I visit Germany, I love it more.' Being asked to repudiate this, Colonel House had refused to do so. Now, more than ever, anything that could for a moment lift the Anglo-American spirit cried out to be discreetly passed on to Henry James. It would be something on a new level of 'I.P.' (as we used to say for 'intensely private') to whisper to Mr.

James that when the British Foreign Minister and President Wilson's closest friend were too weary and worn for other company, they would fore-gather here in the room where I was lunching and forget their cares in remembering — poetry. 'House knows a great deal of English poetry,' said Sir Edward.

I, in my turn remembered the German papers *Jugend* and *Simplicissimus* that, issue by issue, represented Edward Grey with hoofs and horns, the Foul Fiend Incarnate, day and night plotting the destruction of Mittel Europa.

I could count on the grim smile when Henry James should know how I had sat in torture with a raging tooth hearing the literary taste of Colonel House commended: how, when I thought the painful meal was ended a servant brought in a loaf of bread, a plate of butter (it must have been before the rigours of rationing set in) and a dish full of some strange, sticky-looking, very dark stuff.

Sir Edward looked at me, trying to read delight in my dull face. 'You know of course what that is,' he said. No, I didn't think I did. 'You, a Southerner! Don't you see it's sugar,' and I was to help myself. 'I was sure you would like it!' 'When I was a child . . .' I agreed, while my tooth jumped in anguish. 'House introduced me to this,' said Sir Edward. 'House and I sit with the dish between us, butter our bread thick and pile on the sugar. Yes, you must know House.' He would send him a note.

Henry James would like that picture, those two demi-devils, Mephistopheles Grey and House — Poisoner of the President's mind — meeting in secret to quote Wordsworth, and eat Butterbrod and brown sugar.

*　　*　　*　　*

When, at last, Colonel and Mrs. House appeared on the deck of the *New Amsterdam* it was not to face the risk of sitting down. While they walked all eyes followed them till, from the hardihood of some effort to scrape acquaintance, they retreated and were seen no more that day. The next, or the day after, brought me a note: Sir Edward Grey had 'suggested' and so on.

In the House's sitting room I found my fellow passenger, Henry James, Jun., too discreet a spirit to have told me that his uncle had done for him what Sir Edward had for me. As the quiet-mannered host came forward I repressed the desire to greet him with 'Wordsworth and Brown Sugar,' instead of the more obvious; 'So glad to have this opportunity —' But that was not right, either. The faint shadow of wariness that fell across his cordiality told the dread use too often made of such 'Opportunity' — 'to meet a countryman.' I hurried on, 'who does not come from the East, or the North, or the West, as they all seem to. Why do Southerners so seldom come to England?' The shadow passed. I heard a good deal in the next days, about the South, and old Civil War excitements in running the cotton blockade.

The handsome and gracious lady, Colonel House's wife, seemed to care less about walking than her husband did; so it fell out that he and I now and then did a constitutional that gave me, besides pleasure, a sense of useful-

ness as buffer between my companion and a
considerable portion of the passenger list. But
no hint of what contribution, to the dreadful problem, Colonel House was taking home.
He did say one or two things about the President, which won me by what I took for their
modesty. With astonishment I heard, that the
'other self' through whose eyes the President
looked at Europe in the death-grip was not a tried
old friend, but a new element in Wilson's life.
Colonel House told how the friendship had come
about and went on, with what I did not recognize as his never-sleeping diplomacy, to repudiate
the enormous influence he was believed to have
over the President. The popular idea of his advisory relation to Wilson, Colonel House declared,
was pure invention. 'The President does not need
advice. He wants facts. When I land I shall not
go direct to Washington. I shall wait in New York
till I am sent for. The first time I see President
Wilson he will have a half sheet of paper before
him.' Gravely he sketched the President: 'In Berlin did you find. . . . ?' 'Was Burian in Vienna
when . . . ?' No comment on my answers, but
on with the next. At the end, without any discussion, he will pocket the half sheet and begin
to talk home affairs. He may never refer again to
my European journey. But he will have got out
of it all he needed.'

Colonel House's confidence in my not making
too much of 'Opportunity' increased as we neared
New York. He asked one or two questions. I said
I agreed with Henry James that the hospitals, with
all their suffering, were the brightest places in the
darkness over there. It was not only the wounded

who profited but those who worked among them. . . .

I still knew no more than the infant in the steerage about Colonel House's war views or even his race sympathies. But — like so many — I had come to feel at home with 'the Sphinx in the slouch hat.' I accepted it that he, naturally, was not going to tell me how he stood related to the great struggle. But there was no reason to disguise where I stood. I told how I saw, now, that to risk wiping out the things that England stood for, was to risk the best that civilization had won. And I would not allow people to say that my view was prejudiced because the people I had the good fortune to know best, were 'not the average.' For I had seen the average too; and the below-average. It had come my way to know the plain people of many countries; and the point was: they were the vast majority. I could compare and contrast them. There, at the Endell Street Military Hospital, were all sorts and conditions, but mostly what are called the rougher sort. Among the others were men such as I had not known could exist in England. Men who could not write, men who could not read. I knew, for I had read letters for them and written them. They were men from the pithead and the slums, longshoremen and dockers and vagrants. The authorities had said that in a hospital officered by women, the trouble would be to maintain discipline. They added handsomely 'men doctors and surgeons cannot always do that.' In Endell Street the sick and wounded privates did it. Their idea was that when women were in charge it wasn't fair to make a row.

The situation cannot be realized without

knowing something we did not at first faintly suspect. Nearly all those men thought in the early days that they had been turned over to women doctors because there was no hope. Endell Street — merely a place to die in. But they did not wait till the women saved their lives before those rough men showed that they were *decent* people — decent in Henry James's use of the word as well as in the older sense. They expected so little! Yet I have known them show a feeling for good manners, a thought-out considerateness that — one can hardly speak about.

Only little by little we came to understand. Their point of view seemed to be that, for instance, it was unpleasant enough for the nurses to have to listen to some of the chaps who didn't know what they were saying. Those of us who were not indispensable — only helpers at odd jobs, librarians and so on, would be quietly warned by a voice from the nearest bed not to go to the other end of the ward, to-night. So-and-so had come back from his first outing: "'e's been with 'is friends' — in plain English, blind drunk and obscene. Awful ruffians among them of course. Some of them criminals, I daresay. But what one will not forget was the concern we found among those wounded and dying people not to give extra trouble. If we forgot to bring something we had promised, a newspaper, cigarettes, a message — 'do you think,' I asked Colonel House, 'do you think they would remind us?' They knew those lifts too full already, what with Theatre cases, convoy and the rest — they knew the long stone flights we climbed. The soldiers waited till next day. I told about one or two of them ... 'Did I say their country had done nothing for them? I was wrong. If I had never known any English but those I had known in the Endell Street Military Hospital, I should know where my sympathies in the war must be. I should know that this race puts a mark on her poorest that means something beyond price. They may not be able to read but they have their share of — I don't know what else to call it but civilization of the spirit. And that is the stake the world has in Old England.'

Out of the quiet came the quiet voice: 'Those incidents — you have put them into form?' I stared. 'You have written them?' No, I had lived them — 'there was no time to write.' 'There is, now,' he said. 'Besides,' I went on, 'those things are a blessed commonplace. Everybody knows them.' '*Our* people don't,' he said. 'You ought to tell those things to America.' I caught my breath. For I knew, now, the answer to the question every soul on board wanted to put to Colonel House, the answer many souls — one soul more than most — over in England, would want to hear.

It was many a year since Henry James had adjured me to bring him back from France a 'lapful of history and picture;' long since he had written 'Do keep the story fresh and fair for yours ever so yearningly,' longer still since he had asked: 'Write me something good and strong and comfortable.' However I may have failed him then, I need not fail him now. For the whole little episode up to the end had an air of being meant for him.

Colonel House brought the matter up again. If I was not able to do Hospital Sketches, he said, 'do an article.' Not even my failure to see eye to eye with him about military preparedness, put

297

him off, though I had praised England precisely for *not* being prepared for war. I had made it part of her claim on the rest of the world. 'Better do your article,' said Colonel House. In an unaccountable access of courage — 'Would you godfather it,' I said. He smiled; he thought he could see that it came under the favourable notice of the editor of the *New York Times*.

One of the first things I would do on landing would be to 'tell Henry James.' And if the article ever should see print, he must have it. . . .

His nephew and I stood together at the ship's side as the *New Amsterdam* steamed into New York harbour. We looked out over Staten Island, known to Henry James in his youth, and the first of all my remembered playgrounds. Now, the great ship drew into the slip; the gangway went down and several among the waiting crowd pressed on board. Two or three men appeared and drew my companion aside. He came back to me presently. 'They have sent to tell me, uncle Henry is dead.'

I knew the war had killed him as truly as though he had died in the trenches.

# APPENDIX

*'The Article,' as Colonel House had called it, that was to have gone to Henry James, was published in the* NEW YORK TIMES *March 11, 1916.*

To the Editor:

Since I was in America a year ago I have seen the birth of a new England. Through the earlier months of the war there was not, even among the expert few, the faintest realization of what the struggle was to be, either in time or intensity.

One word about this same unpreparedness, for it is perhaps England's highest distinction, and most valid claim upon the democracies of the world.

Consider the 'stuff' for the war she had at command, and her past military record. She might have made war what Mirabeau says her enemies have made of it: 'a national industry.' To such an extent had she abandoned the art, that she needed time and suffering to relearn the old barbarous lessons.

Until August, 1914, England was otherwise occupied. At home she was cultivating the arts of peace and broadening the democratic basis. For what is the outstanding political fact of English history since 1813 but an increasing collaboration between the governors and the governed, an increasing number of the people bidden to 'share' in public affairs?

If that has been her business at home, what was she

about abroad? Besides carrying on her commerce, which filled the ports and populated all the seas, she was occupied in such feats of government as preparing and conferring a constitution upon a conquered people in South Africa; in meeting the complex claims entailed by her responsibilities in India, Egypt, and the colonies, and in discharging her responsibilities in such a way as made those distant populations fly to her aid with money and with men, in their tens of thousands, to defend her and to die for her.

England herself expected no such proof of the success of those activities to which she had devoted herself during the time the enemy was arming for her destruction. But the enemy has seen, with undisguised amazement, the vindication of her genius for administration and the evidence of her power for inspiring love and faith.

In the liberties England has conferred on her dependencies we seem to see her realization that the dominion of force, however triumphant at any given time, is never a safe dominion. There is, in a mutable world like ours, a practical certainty that a yet greater force will arrive to drive the victor of yesterday out of the field. A mere question of time. There is no safety under heaven except in voluntary co-operation.

To any one like myself, who has been much in Germany and loved her literature and many of her people, there is no shadow of doubt as to their great power to serve mankind. Their tragic failure is, in essence, a lack of faith. Germany would dragoon the people into order and prosperity. She will do anything for them under heaven except trust them.

To make people responsible by giving them responsibility, to induce the spirit of voluntary co-operation, was England's contribution to the world. You are in contact with the civilizing effect of that quality every hour you live among her people.

Not to dwell on the gentle manners of the great mass

of the population, you feel the spirit of co-operation at work in the most visible sign of the arm of the law. The policeman in England is your friend. He is the public's friend. In Germany he is your enemy and the public's enemy. Rude, tyrannical, hated by his own townsfolk, he is the symbol not of good sense and civic co-operation, but of despotism, as though he were intent on carrying out the idea expressed by the Kaiser in a speech made soon after his accession: 'One only is master within the empire, and I will tolerate no other.' The German policeman conveys to you that you are to do this or that not because it is reasonable and for the common good, but because obedience is your first business. As I have private cause to know, and as a publicist has recently said: with the German, terror, not sense of justice, is held to be the best security for obedience. If that view should prevail, the men of the future will not find themselves inheritors of thousands of years of progress; they will find themselves back at the starting-point of civilization. The question for us to answer is: shall we follow the leader in this retreat to cave conditions? For you may call the new coercion 'high explosive,' 'airship,' or what you like. It is the old savagery with a new face.

In England you see to-day the expression of the spirit of co-operation in the greatest voluntary army that history has known. And you will see the same principle in a more impressive spectacle: a whole great nation enrolled for service. At the ghastly price of war, a new kind of socialism has been attained.

Service has become the badge of honour, and idleness disgrace. To give — work or treasure or life — is the common passion.

The week I sailed, a group of moneyed men who formerly fought death-duties and insurance acts, met in London to appoint a deputation to the Prime Minister. The object was to induce Mr. Asquith to bring pressure upon the Chancellor to impose a severer scheme of taxation. The poor give to Funds, give with both hands to the soldiers, give the produce of little poultry runs and cottage gardens to the fleet, and all classes give their sons.

Speaking of a uniform for the First Aid Nursing Yeomanry recently sanctioned by the War Office, a sometime 'smart woman,' now working in a canteen, said: 'Our old clothes are our uniform.' People are ashamed of luxury — even the aged and the ailing are ashamed of idleness. It is an England purged and strengthened by a spirit which reaches out to the limits of the empire.

It is in this changed England that a danger lurks for other nations, the neutral quite as much as the enemy. The rest of the world is too prone to think that because the Englishman was not easily roused he is not thoroughly roused. I find that many Americans have but little idea what England's contribution has been. Apart from what she herself has achieved, she is behind all that the Allies have achieved. But for her, long ago they must have given in.

England's unreadiness in blowing her own trumpet has been misunderstood. It is a busy world, and while everybody has time to criticize, few have time to inform themselves. We misjudge the Englishman's account of himself because we too often judge him by our standards instead of by his own. Just as over-statement is the tendency, if not the habit, of most people, so of the English is understatement. Self-criticism, often self-depreciation, is the form his particular kind of pride takes — often a stingingly effective rebuke to the boastfulness of others.

I repeat, as my special message to my own country, there is danger not only for England's enemies in her old ingrained habit of inarticulateness and her new, her very new, reaction to the crisis in which she found herself in the second year of the war.

No unprejudiced eye can have watched the transformation the last year has made without realizing it is idle to expect that a people like these English, rich and luxurious, who yet can voluntarily assume poverty, voluntarily accept hardship, will be brought to consider a peace which is ineffectual, or which is unfair, whether toward herself or her allies.

England will fight on.

The outside world very imperfectly understands her resources, her strength of resistance, above all, her power of enduring. There is no price her destiny can demand of her which she will not pay for free institutions.

I do not say she is invincible — I know nothing about that. I go only so far as to ask: What price are the free countries of the world prepared to see England pay for the crime of failing to tax the pockets, and the free spirits of her people with the maintenance of a great military system? Are the democracies of the world prepared to see her bleed to death for that?

What lover of free institutions who knows modern Germany can think of her triumph without knowing his dearest beliefs in danger?

In danger? In peril of extinction for generations to come!

Yours, &c.,
Elizabeth Robins.